£11.99

THE HOLOCAUST

Art, Music and Writings from the Holocaust

Susan Willoughby

Heinemann
LIBRARY

www.heinemann.co.uk/library

Visit our website to find out more information about **Heinemann Library** books.

To order:
☎ Phone 44 (0) 1865 888066
🖹 Send a fax to 44 (0) 1865 314091
💻 Visit the Heinemann Bookshop at www.heinemann.co.uk/library to browse our catalogue and order online.

First published in Great Britain by Heinemann Library, Halley Court, Jordan Hill, Oxford, OX2 8EJ, part of Harcourt Education.
Heinemann is a registered trademark of Harcourt Education Ltd.

Editorial: Andrew Farrow and Dan Nunn
Design: David Poole and Tinstar Design Limited (www.tinstar.co.uk)
Illustrations by Martin Griffin
Picture Research: Maria Joannou and Thelma Gilbert
Production: Viv Hichens

Originated by Ambassador Litho Ltd
Printed in China by Wing King Tong

ISBN 0 431 15370 1
07 06 05 04 03
10 9 8 7 6 5 4 3 2 1

British Library Cataloguing in Publication Data
Willoughby, Susan
    Art, Music and Writings from the Holocaust. - (The Holocaust) 1. Holocaust, Jewish (1939-1945) - Juvenile literature 2. World War, 1939-1945 - Art and the war - Juvenile literature 3. World War, 1939-1945 - Literature and the war - Juvenile literature 4. World War, 1939-1945 - Music and the war - Juvenile literature
    I. Title
    940.5'318
A full catalogue record for this book is available from the British Library.

Acknowledgements
The publishers would like to thank the following for permission to reproduce photographs: AKG London pp. **9**, **10**, **11**; Art Collection, Ghetto Fighters House Museum (Beit Lohamei Haghetaot Museum), Israel/Yair Pelieg pp. **19**, **49**; Beate Klarsfeld Foundation/David Olere pp. **4**, **5**, **13**, **38**; Deutsches Historishes Museum p. **15**; Florida Center for Instructional Technology/Dr Roy Winkelman pp. **36**, **37**; Hulton Getty Picture Collection p. **16**; Kurt Jiri Kotouc & Marie Rut Krizkova/George Brady pp. **43** (top), **43** (bottom); Mary Evans Picture Library p. **6**; Mervyn Peake p. **39**; Mezcenstwo Walka and Zaglada Zydow Polsce, courtesy of Florida Center for Instructional Technology pp. **28**, **29**; Narodni Filmovy Archiv p. **44**; Randall Bytwerk, CAS Department, Calvin College p. **12**; Scott Sakansky/Florida Center for Instructional Technology p. **40**; Terezín Memorial pp. **45**, **46**; Thomas Haas p. **47**; University Library, Jerusalem p. **24**; USHMM pp. **7**, **8**, **17**, **25**, **26**, **30**, **32**, **34**, **35**; Yad Vashem pp. **14**, **20**, **21**, **22**, **23**, **27**

The pictures on pages **22** and **23** are taken from the album *The Legend of Ghetto Lodz, 1940–44*, Gouache, ink and pencil on paper. (Jasny Collection, gift of Chara Jasny. Courtesy of the Yad Vashem Art Museum, Jerusalem.)

Cover photograph reproduced with the permission of Alexandre Olère.

The publishers would like to thank Jonathan Gorsky of the Council of Christians and Jews for his assistance in the preparation of this book.

Every effort has been made to contact copyright holders of any material reproduced in this book. Any omissions will be rectified in subsequent printings if notice is given to the publishers.

Disclaimer
All the Internet addresses (URLs) given in this book were valid at the time of going to press. However, due to the dynamic nature of the Internet, some addresses may have changed, or sites may have ceased to exist since publication. While the author and publishers regret any inconvenience this may cause readers, no responsibility for any such changes can be accepted by either the author or the publishers.

Contents

Words appearing in the text in bold, **like this**, are explained in the Glossary.

Witnesses to the Holocaust

Between 1941 and 1945, thousands of men, women and children were **transported** from eastern Europe to a place called Auschwitz-Birkenau, in Poland. They travelled for many days by train in over-crowded cattle trucks with very little water and even less food. Upon arrival, as the wide truck doors were slid back, they were greeted by the sight of guards with guns, whips and dogs. Able-bodied men, women and older children were separated out to swell the ranks of forced-labour gangs or to become human guinea pigs for medical experimentation. The sick, elderly and women with small children and babies were marched immediately to specially built **gas chambers** where they were murdered.

All were victims of the Holocaust. This was the planned and systematic murder of well over six million people carried out on the orders of Adolf Hitler by the **Nazis**, mainly between 1940 and 1945. The vast majority – nine in every ten – were **Jews**, but **Gypsies**, **Jehovah's Witnesses**, the mentally and physically handicapped, **homosexuals** and **Slavs** were also amongst this unimaginably vast number.

Unable to Work

Prisoners who arrived at Auschwitz were separated into those fit for hard labour and those too young, old or weak to work. This painting by David Olère, called *Unable to Work* (1945), captures the sad image of those too weak, old or young to work being sent to their deaths in the gas chambers.

Terrible scenes

After he was liberated, David Olère painted some of the terrible scenes that he had witnessed and kept in his memory, including this one. Unlike many Jews, David survived because the Nazis made use of his artistic talents.

Auschwitz evidence

Auschwitz-Birkenau was just one of six **death camps** created to carry out Hitler's '**Final Solution**' – the complete extermination of Jews and other **undesirables**. Yet Auschwitz is the one that has come to symbolize the Holocaust. This may be because so many people – 1.25 million – lost their lives there and the camp remains as evidence of the terrible things that happened there. We also have many spoken and written records from survivors of Auschwitz, and the experiences of those who died are captured in the work of artists, poets and writers.

David Olère – artist of death

David Olère was born in Warsaw, Poland in 1902. He was an artist from an early age. He was working in France as a professional artist when the Nazis invaded in 1939. Along with thousands of French Jews, he was eventually arrested and transported to Auschwitz-Birkenau in February 1943. There he became a ***Sonderkommando***, a member of a special work force that was made to empty the gas chambers and transport the bodies to the **crematoria** for burning. Normally, this work force was changed every three or four months and the men were sent to the gas chambers themselves. Unlike most of the others, he survived. He was saved from death by his artistic ability. He drew and illustrated postcards for the Nazi officers and translated radio broadcasts. David's work is very important because there are no photographs of what happened in the gas chambers.

What was the Holocaust?

To understand how the Holocaust came about we must go back to 1933 when Adolf Hitler and the Nazi Party came to power in Germany. Germany had been defeated in the First World War, which ended in 1918. Then, between 1918 and 1933, Germany became a **democracy** known as the Weimar Republic. However, the country's parliament failed to bring about economic recovery in Germany and, by 1932, the country was in the grip of a deep **depression**. Over 6 million people were unemployed. It was a desperate situation that opened the way for extremists to come to power.

The rise of Adolf Hitler and the Nazis

Adolf Hitler claimed to have the answers to Germany's problems. The German people were won over by his confident promises of **prosperity**. He raised their spirits by telling them that they were members of a 'master race' that would soon rule the world. He told them that their armies had been betrayed into surrendering at the end of the First World War. People voted for his Nazi Party in the **Reichstag** elections of 1932 and Hitler became Chancellor (a kind of Prime Minister) in 1933. By 1934, he had been given the power to become a **dictator**.

A pure race

Hitler said that this German master race must be made up of pure **Aryans**. He believed that the Aryan race was superior to all other races, and that it must be kept pure at all costs. Hitler knew that **anti-Semitism** was common in post-war Germany, so when he blamed the Jews for Germany's troubles, people believed him.

Adolf Hitler

Hitler was born in Austria, in 1889. After the First World War, he became involved in politics. In 1925, his book, *Mein Kampf*, was published. In it he wrote about his belief in the superiority of the Aryan race and the inferiority of Jews.

Euthanasia

From 1940, the Nazis carried out a **euthanasia programme** to kill off handicapped children and adults. They were seen as a threat to the strength and purity of Germany and had to be 'removed'. This was the beginning of mass murder using gas or lethal injections. It gave the Nazis the idea for how the '**Final Solution**' could be carried out. Hartheim Castle in Austria (seen here) was one of the killing centres.

Of course, not all Germans supported Hitler. Many lost their lives for criticizing him and for attempting to end his cruel regime. Many others opposed him but were too afraid to criticize him openly.

While the Jews felt the full force of Hitler's racism, others also suffered. Jehovah's witnesses, homosexuals, the mentally and physically handicapped, Gypsies and, later, the Slav people of eastern Europe, all became victims of Nazi persecution.

Persecution, discrimination and slaughter

In the years between 1933 and 1939, Jews in Germany were persecuted, deprived of their property and their rights, sent to **concentration camps**, beaten and murdered. Children suffered as they were expelled from their schools, separated from their friends and often their own families.

As Hitler's armies moved across Europe after 1939, Jews were rounded up and put into camps. In eastern Europe, mobile killing squads – the **Einsatzgruppen** – wiped out thousands of Jews, Gypsies and other 'undesirables' in mass executions. Jews were forced to enter **ghettos**. There they lived in filth, squalor and daily terror of **transportation**. Most of those people transported were never seen again, as the Nazis carried out their 'Final Solution'.

Artistic responses

These terrifying experiences produced an amazing outpouring of art, poetry and writing. Many found that they could only express their feelings of pain, bewilderment and loss through poetry, painting, drawing or writing. Many used their talents deliberately to make sure that they left behind a record of the things that the Nazis had done. This was the only way that they could protest.

The culture of Nazism

Even during the difficult days after the First World War, Berlin was regarded as one of the cultural centres of Europe. It was renowned for its scholars, art collections and music. However, when the **Nazis** came to power they banned the work of some writers, musicians and artists whose work they considered to be '**degenerate**'. On the other hand, Hitler wanted to maintain the impression that Germans enjoyed a rich cultural life. This was part of his **propaganda** programme, as was the art, music and writing that he approved.

'Degenerate' culture

In Berlin today, in the square in front of the Opera, an unusual memorial can be found. It consists of a pane of glass set in the ground. Looking down into the depths beneath, only empty bookshelves can be seen. Beside it is a plaque, which reads: 'Wherever books are burnt, men will eventually be burnt.'

The memorial marks the place where, on 10 May 1933, thousands of books were publicly burned. As they were thrown into the fire by Stormtroopers (the Nazi Party's private army, also known as the 'Brown shirts') and pro-Nazi students, the names of the undesirable authors were read out. It was like an execution. For many, it must have been an alarming sight as books by respected scholars and writers such as Albert Einstein, Sigmund Freud, Ernest Hemingway and Sinclair Lewis went up in flames. They were declared undesirable either because their authors were **Jewish** or because they promoted ideas and lifestyles of which the Nazis disapproved. They were described as 'degenerate'. At midnight, Joseph Goebbels (Hitler's 'Minister of Propaganda and Public Enlightenment') arrived at the scene and delivered a stirring speech hailing the dawn of a new era. But what kind of era would it be?

Bertold Brecht – a 'degenerate' playwright

Bertold Brecht was a playwright who openly criticized Hitler. His work was banned and he escaped from Germany in 1933. He returned in 1948 and became recognized as one of Germany's greatest writers.

Acceptable literature

Around 2500 writers left Germany in the early years of Nazi rule, in order to be free to write as they pleased. Writers who supported, and who were supported by, the Nazis, replaced them. To the outside world, German literature seemed to be flourishing. Joseph Goebbels' Ministry of Propaganda supervised Germany's 2500 publishing houses, 6000 state libraries and 23,000 bookshops. Three thousand authors made sure that Germans read what the Nazis wanted them to read in the 20,000 books that were published annually. There were fifty prizes awarded each year to reward them for their loyal efforts. However, Hitler's own book, *Mein Kampf* (which translates into English as 'My Struggle'), remained the best seller. He wrote this while he was in prison in 1923. In it he set out his ideas about the superiority of the **Aryan** race. By 1940, six million copies had been sold!

The theatre

A similar fate was suffered by playwrights and actors. Many plays were banned and half of Germany's actors found themselves out of work. Instead, theatres were used to stage large-scale productions glorifying Germany. People were encouraged to go to the theatre with cheap or even half-price tickets, which could be used to see ten plays. However, they were not allowed to choose the play, the date or the place!

The sight of such mass audiences convinced many people in Europe that some kind of cultural revolution was underway in Germany. Shakespeare's plays continued to be performed, particularly *The Merchant of Venice*. This particular play appealed to the Nazis because the character of the Jewish merchant, Shylock, matched the evil and greedy image of a Jew that the Nazis wanted to portray. However, the Nazis still changed the story so that the marriage of Jessica (Shylock's daughter) to Lorenzo, a Christian, was made acceptable to Nazi race laws. They did this by suggesting that Shylock was not really her father!

'Degenerate' art and music

It was not only books that the **Nazis** destroyed. In 1939, 4000 paintings, including masterpieces by Paul Cézanne, Pablo Picasso, Vincent Van Gogh, Henri Matisse and Paul Gaugin, were publicly burned. They had been part of an exhibition of '**degenerate**' art in Munich in 1937. It had attracted two million visitors. The Nazis had hoped that they would respond with the same angry reaction as the visitor quoted here:

> 'The artists ought to be tied up next to their pictures so that every German can spit in their faces – but not only the artists, also the museum directors who, at a time of mass unemployment, poured vast sums into the ever open jaws of the perpetrators of these atrocities.'

Hitler disliked all forms of modern art but the work of some artists was also banned because they were **Jewish** or Russian. To him, all Russians were **communists** and **Slavs**. Hitler despised both. For example, the work of the Russian-born artist, Wassily Kandinsky, was banned. Even though he had been born in Russia, Kandinsky lived and worked in Germany. A similar fate befell the work of Marc Chagall. Chagall was born in Russia but spent most of his life in France. His family background was Jewish and this shows up in many of his paintings.

Marc Chagall – a 'degenerate' artist

This painting is called *The Soldier*. It shows the use of bright colour and irregular forms that are typical of Chagall's work. This made it unpopular with Hitler. He also didn't like the influence of Chagall's Russian-Jewish origins on the artist's paintings.

Nazi art

Hitler decided and dictated acceptable artistic styles himself. As a young man, he had studied art in Vienna. He had developed his own style of painting and had attempted, unsuccessfully, to become an artist. He rejected the vivid colours and irregular shapes of modern artists, insisting instead on the use of natural colours and realistic forms. Paintings that he approved of reflected his vision of the perfect German and idealized German life. German painters who produced these ideal works of art were well rewarded financially and looked after. Those who refused to produce art that was acceptable to the Nazis, and wished to remain free to express themselves, were forced to leave Germany or face a life of poverty.

The ideal Germans

This picture portrays the ideal of German country life. The family are shown bearing all the characteristics of Hitler's pure, **Aryan** Germans – fair hair, blue eyes and regular features.

'Degenerate' music

Hitler also had fixed ideas about music. By the 1930s, Germany, and especially the nightclubs of Berlin, had taken in the craze that swept the USA in the 1920s – jazz. Hitler disapproved of this partly because it was loud and brash, but also because it was associated with immorality and it was the music of the black Americans, who were members of an **inferior** race according to Nazi beliefs.

Other musicians and composers were also experimenting with new rhythms and sounds in the early 1930s. Hitler banned this kind of 'modern' music. Several of the banned composers and musicians were also Jews. These included Arnold Schoenberg (composer), Otto Klemperer and Bruno Walter (conductors). They were forced to leave Germany and found refuge in the USA, Britain or elsewhere in Europe. Many Jewish musicians eventually perished in the **gas chambers** of the death camps.

Acceptable music

Hitler loved music that glorified Germany. His favourite composers were Richard Wagner and Ludwig van Beethoven. Richard Strauss and Carl Orff were employed to compose music for the Olympic Games in Berlin in 1936. Much of the music composed for the Nazis was marching music. Folk music and dancing were popular with the **Nazi Youth**, who also formed choirs and orchestras. Operettas and ballets were performed in Berlin throughout the war years.

Nazi culture and the Jews

Stolen treasures

Hitler built up a huge art collection for himself. It was his intention to make his birthplace, the town of Linz in northern Austria, the art capital of the world. As the German armies swept across Europe after 1939, art galleries were looted and the stolen treasures taken back to Germany. Both Hitler and Goebbels had huge private collections of stolen works of art worth millions of pounds.

Art as propaganda

Art played an important part in Hitler's **anti-Semitic propaganda**. While artists were ordered to paint beautiful portraits of **Aryan** Germans, they were required to show **Jews** as ugly and distasteful. The pictures were designed to encourage fear, suspicion and revulsion. Such images became part of everyday life. Children saw them in their schoolbooks. They appeared in newspapers such as *Der Stürmer* and on posters in public places. Through this kind of constant exposure, many Germans were persuaded to believe what Hitler was saying about the Jews.

Painting and playing to survive

While the **Nazis** 'cleansed' Europe of the art, music and writing of Jews, they were happy to make use of Jewish talents in the **concentration camps**. For many artists and musicians, this meant they could avoid hard labour and in some, though not all, cases survive. For example, David Olère (*see page* 5) survived because he wrote letters for Nazi officers and decorated them with flowers. He was also a scholar. He spoke six languages including English, French and Russian. This made him useful as a translator.

Anti-Semitic art

This illustration from a children's book is called *The Experience of Hans and Else with a Strange Man*. The caption says, 'Here kids, I have some candy for you. But you both have to come with me.' It shows the Jew as a threat to Aryan children. It is deliberately designed to encourage children to fear and hate Jews.

Dinah Gottlieb

Dinah Gottlieb was born in Czechoslovakia. Before the war, she studied graphics and sculpture. She was taken, with her mother, to the Terezín **ghetto** and from there in September 1943 to Auschwitz **death camp**. She was fortunate because, unlike most, her **transport** was not sent straight to the gas chambers.

At first she was made to work at hard labour, lifting heavy rocks. However, her artistic talent was noticed by one of the officers and she was given the task of painting the slogan '*Arbeit Macht Frei*' ('work liberates') on walls all over the camp. Soon her drawings were in demand by Nazi officers. She came to the attention of Joseph Mengele, the chief doctor of the camp and the man responsible for carrying out horrific medical experiments. She spent most of the remaining time in the camp drawing his victims on his orders. This was to help him with his research into inherited characteristics. When most of the other Czech inmates were sent to the gas chambers in 1944, Dinah and her mother were among a very small number who were spared. Dinah's artistic ability saved her life.

Playing to live

It is hard to imagine that among the starved, **emaciated** faces of the inmates of Auschwitz, Bergen-Belsen and other camps were some of Europe's most talented musicians. The Nazi officers took advantage of this. Camp orchestras were formed and were ordered to entertain them. Cruelly, they were also used to 'welcome' new arrivals to the camps as the cattle trucks carrying them drew into the sidings. At Auschwitz, the orchestra was ordered to play while naked women and children queued up to be herded into the **gas chambers**.

Painting to survive

David Olère drew this picture of himself shortly after his liberation from Auschwitz. It is called *For a Crust of Bread*. In it he shows himself writing and illustrating a letter for which he was rewarded with a crust of bread.

Persecution and rejection

As we have seen, when Hitler came to power, his attack on the **Jews** and other 'misfits' was swift. By 1935, most Jews were no longer free to own businesses, practise medicine, mix freely with non-Jewish Germans or marry them. Mixed marriages were declared unlawful and families were split up. Jewish children were humiliated in their schools. Their friendships with non-Jewish children were destroyed. Jews were also deprived of their German nationality – they became stateless people.

After 1938, large numbers of German and Austrian Jews attempted to find new and safer homes in other lands. Some were successful, but most were refused entry to countries like the USA, Britain and Canada, whose governments wanted to restrict **immigration**. Many of those who went to other European countries, such as Belgium and the Netherlands, were eventually imprisoned by the Nazis after 1939. Their sense of rejection and isolation is shown in paintings and writings of the time.

Felix Nussbaum (1904–44)

Felix was born in Osnabrück, Germany in 1904. The experience of his family is an example of the struggle to find a safe home shared by thousands of German Jewish families after 1933. Felix studied art in Berlin, where his paintings were exhibited. When Hitler came to power, Felix fled to Italy to escape **persecution**. His parents left Osnabrück in search of safety and joined their son in Italy. However, they soon felt homesick and returned to Germany. Felix then moved to Belgium, where he thought he could paint freely. After the German **occupation** of Belgium in 1940, he was arrested and sent to a camp at Saint Cyprien in southern France. He escaped and lived in hiding, but continued to paint. His powerful paintings show his fear for his people and his feelings of isolation and persecution. Finally, Felix, his wife and son were arrested and sent to Auschwitz, where they died in August 1944. His paintings survived because they were left behind when he was **transported** to Auschwitz.

No place of refuge

In this painting, Felix Nussbaum captures the fear and despair of a Jewish refugee. He has no place of refuge anywhere in the world, symbolized by the globe. He is in a narrow, bare, prison-like room. His only possessions are in a small bundle at his side. This is one of a number of his pictures that tell the story of the Jewish people and their sufferings.

Threesome

Felix Nussbaum painted this picture of himself, his wife Felka and his son Jaqui in hiding in January 1944. This was one of his last pictures. In it he tries to capture the plight of Jews, quietly enduring persecution, afraid but still hopeful.

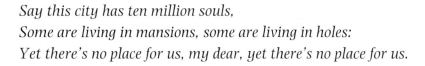

Refugee Blues

The mood of Felix Nussbaum's painting of the refugee on page 14 is reflected in the words of a poem called *Refugee Blues* by the English poet, W. H. Auden, written in March 1939. Auden was living in Berlin at the time when Hitler rose to power. He left Europe for America in 1939.

> *Say this city has ten million souls,*
> *Some are living in mansions, some are living in holes:*
> *Yet there's no place for us, my dear, yet there's no place for us.*
>
> *Once we had a country and we thought it fair,*
> *Look in the atlas and you'll find it there:*
> *We cannot go there now, my dear, we cannot go there now...*
>
> *Thought I heard the thunder rumbling in the sky;*
> *It was Hitler over Europe, saying 'They must die':*
> *O we were in his mind, my dear, O we were in his mind.*
>
> *Saw a poodle in a jacket fastened with a pin,*
> *Saw a door opened and a cat let in:*
> *But they weren't German Jews, my dear, but they weren't German Jews...*
>
> *Stood on a great plain in the falling snow;*
> *Ten thousand soldiers marched to and fro:*
> *Looking for you and me, my dear, looking for you and me.*

Five verses from *Refugee Blues* by W. H. Auden

The diary of Anne Frank

Anne Frank was born in Frankfurt, Germany in 1929. Her father, Otto, took the family to Amsterdam in the Netherlands in 1933 to escape **Nazi persecution**. After the German invasion of the Netherlands in 1940, Anne's life changed. The **Jewish** family were forced to go into hiding to avoid arrest. During this time, Anne kept a diary. Her daily accounts of life in Amsterdam help us to see what it was like for young Jews living under Nazi rule. In 1944, the family was betrayed and their hiding place was raided by the Nazis. Anne was sent to Auschwitz and then to Bergen-Belsen where she died of **typhus**.

The voyage of the *St Louis*

In May 1939, the *St Louis* set sail from Hamburg carrying 960 Jewish passengers. They had bought tickets to carry them to Havana, Cuba and **visas** to gain entry. The voyage began with optimism and excitement. It ended in tragedy. When they arrived at Havana, they were refused entry. Among them were many children including thirteen-year-old Liesel Joseph, who has left behind her image of life on board the ship during this difficult time. Eventually, a small number were allowed to land. The ship was then forced to return to Europe. Those who were allowed to land in France, Belgium and the Netherlands were put in camps. Very few of the passengers survived the Holocaust.

An extract from Anne Frank's diary

Saturday, 20 June 1942.
[Anne tells 'Kitty', her diary, the story of her life so far:]

'After May, 1940, good times rapidly fled: first the war, then the **capitulation**, followed by the arrival of the Germans. That was when the sufferings of us Jews really began. Anti-Jewish decrees followed each other in quick succession. Jews must wear a yellow star, Jews must hand in their bicycles, Jews are banned from trams and forbidden to drive. Jews are only allowed to do their shopping between three and five o'clock and then only in shops which bear the placard 'Jewish shop'. Jews must be indoors by eight o'clock and cannot even sit in their gardens after that hour... Jews may not visit Christians, Jews must go to Jewish schools, and many more restrictions.'

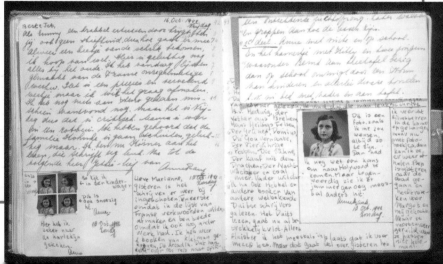

August 3th 1939

THE GERMAN SHIP "St.LOUIS" FROM: HABANA TO ANTW

Liesl Joseph
LONDON
11 years ENGL...

The letters of Julius Hermann

Julius Hermann was another passenger on the *St Louis*. After the ship returned to Europe, he landed in France and was placed in an **internment camp** at Saint Cyprien, near the Spanish border – this was before the German invasion. In this extract from one of his letters to his relatives in the USA, he provides a very clear picture of his suffering:

'All the clothes, underwear and other articles of use that were to come with us have all been lost... You can imagine that the squalor that you see here makes the situation worse. Typhus and malaria, as well as lice, fleas, and tremendous hordes of flies, give you a sense of it. Sand is a foot deep, and we are dreading the coming storms which will blow the sand into the cracks of our temporary barracks... Rats and mice also seek refuge in our housing when the weather gets colder... These conditions are almost unbearable.

'When one read and heard earlier travel descriptions from prison camps, etc., about the conditions there, one viewed all this as impossible. Now, when one has to experience this oneself, the question needs to be posed, how can this happen in the 20th century?'

Julius was deported to Auschwitz in August 1942, where he died. His wife, daughter and other relatives, from whom he had been separated since 1935, were sent to the Riga **ghetto** (in Latvia) where they too almost certainly died.

On board the *St Louis*

Liesel Joseph was on board the *St Louis*. In her picture, the bright sky expresses her hope for the future. The dark and gloomy ship, without any signs of life on board, shows the anxiety and despair that must have overwhelmed the passengers.

Images of ghetto life

As Hitler's invading armies occupied the countries of eastern Europe, the **Nazis** dealt ruthlessly with the large **Jewish** populations. They were either wiped out in mass killings by the ***Einsatzgruppen*** or they were forced to live in **ghettos** – areas of cities or towns that were eventually walled or fenced off to separate Jews and others, including **Gypsies**, from the rest of the population. There were 356 ghettos in Eastern Europe. They became overcrowded, dirty and unhealthy places. Violence and cruelty were parts of everyday life and the people lived in constant fear of death or **deportation**. Perhaps one of the worst features was that the Nazis gave the responsibility for running the ghettos to a Jewish council. Jewish policemen ensured that the rules were kept.

A Jewish committee drew up the list of people to be deported. So it sometimes seemed that many of the terrible things that happened to Jews were carried out by Jews themselves. The bitterness that this caused is seen in some of the writings that came from the ghettos and camps. By 1945, only a small proportion of ghetto dwellers had survived to speak of their experiences. However, the diaries, poetry and vivid pictures and paintings of those who vanished leave us with a deeper insight into the reality of life in the ghettos. They also show us very clearly that people managed to maintain an amazingly rich cultural life in the face of such hardship.

Jewish ghettos

This map shows the locations of the main Jewish ghettos in Nazi occupied Europe, 1941–42.

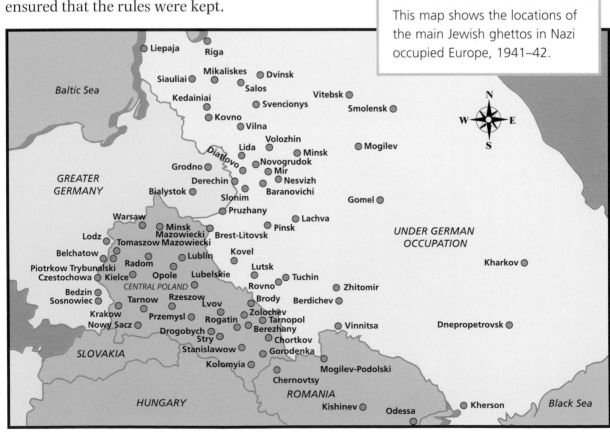

The entrance to the Lodz ghetto

This painting, by an artist in the Lodz ghetto in Poland, shows Jews arriving with their belongings at the entrance to the ghetto.

Isaac Katzenelson

Isaac Katzenelson was born in the former Soviet Union in 1886 but grew up in Warsaw, Poland. When Hitler began to send Polish Jews to the ghettos and camps, he escaped to France. He was arrested and put in a **concentration camp** at Vittel. From there he was deported to Auschwitz where he died. His poem has since been set to music:

*I looked out of the window and beheld the
    hands that struck;
Observed who did the beating up, and who
    were beaten up;
And wrung my hands for very shame... oh
    mockery and shame:
It was by Jews, alas, by Jews my Jewish folk
    was slain!...*

*They tore the doors down, tore inside with
    curses and commands;
Invaded Jewish homes with clubs held ready
    in their hands;
Found us and beat us, bullied us to where the
    wagons stood –
Both young and old! And soiled the light of day,
    and spat at God...*

*The German stands apart, as if he's laughing
    at the scene –
The German keeps his distance – has no need
    to come between;
Ah, woe is me! He's managed it! By Jews my
    Jews are slain!
Behold the wagons! Ah, behold the agony, the
    shame.*

Three verses from *The Song of the Slaughtered Jewish People* by Isaac Katzenelson

The Lodz ghetto

The two largest ghettos in eastern Europe were in Poland – Warsaw, the biggest, and then Lodz. Lodz was the last ghetto to be destroyed. Its inmates left behind a vast amount of information about what had happened during their time there. Much of this was in the form of paintings, diaries and poetry. The Lodz ghetto was surrounded by a wooden fence and barbed wire. Once inside, Jews were not allowed to leave on penalty of death. German soldiers guarded the outside, Jewish ghetto police guarded the inside.

A concert party

It is hard to imagine that the happy, smiling faces of this group of actors, like others in the Lodz ghetto, lived in overcrowded and unhealthy conditions and in constant fear.

As time went by, the inmates became exhausted by hard labour and weak from hunger and disease. Of the 233,000 who entered the ghetto in 1939, only 164,000 remained by May 1940. In spite of this, music, theatre, art, concerts and educational lectures were very much part of life in the ghetto. The inmates were determined to retain some dignity and quality of life in the face of degradation and humiliation. This also happened in most of the other ghetto communities, such as those at Kovno (in Lithuania), Warsaw (in Poland) and Terezín (near Prague in Czechoslovakia).

Music, writing and drama

Drama and songs did not just help people in the ghettos maintain some pride and quality of life. They also preserved their traditions, religion and culture. Study, writing and songs also helped people to deal with much of their despair, anger and frustration. Laughter played an important part, even though the humour was often bitter and sarcastic. Music was very important, too. Musicians and composers in the ghettos wrote new lyrics to old songs so that the inmates could sing out their defiance.

Photographs from the ghetto show street singers surrounded by children and adults. Artists portrayed musicians playing in coffee- and tea-houses where everyone joined in. Small orchestras or quartets performed regularly. Photographs and drawings also survive of ghetto productions with costumes and specially designed scenery. Creativity seems to have provided some compensation for the lack of food and the indignities that ghetto dwellers had to endure. Reading, writing and studying stimulated minds and kept alive the hope of a return to normality.

A song from the Warsaw ghetto

Let us be jolly and share good jokes
We'll yet sit shiva * when Hitler croaks.
Biri-bi, bam-bam-bam
(Repeat the chorus)
Let us take comfort, forget our sorrow;
Through Hitler's body the worms will burrow.
(Chorus)
Who drive us now to Treblinka's horror
Themselves will be under the ground tomorrow
(Chorus)
Arm in arm, we'll yet make merry
And dance through a German cemetery.

* To 'sit shiva' is a Jewish mourning ritual.

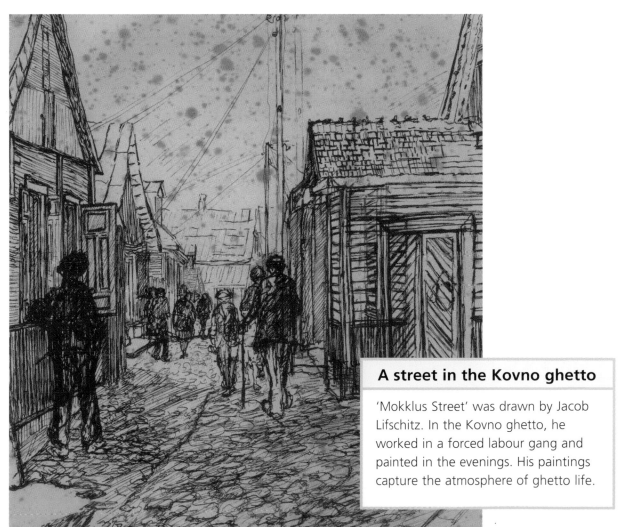

A street in the Kovno ghetto

'Mokklus Street' was drawn by Jacob Lifschitz. In the Kovno ghetto, he worked in a forced labour gang and painted in the evenings. His paintings capture the atmosphere of ghetto life.

Children of the ghettos

Within the ghettos, adults did their utmost to make sure that children were sheltered from the harsh reality of their strange and hostile world. Efforts were made to secure better living conditions and play areas for the children. Providing them with education was a high priority. Schools were set up in the Lodz ghetto during the first two years but as thousands more people arrived, schools were turned into living accommodation instead. A young boy, David Sierakowiak, kept a diary in which he wrote about his school and the quality of what he learned there:

Sunday, April 27, 1941
'Today was the first day of school...
The school is located in a tiny building which can hardly hold our benches. For now there are no other supplies (not even a blackboard). There is no cloakroom, and in the classroom we sit wearing our coats. Today we already had six classes.'

Monday, May 26, 1941
'...We're working now on Cicero's often-praised speech against Cataline, and next week we will start metrics. In mathematics we're doing equations. In other subjects, except German, we are falling behind.'

Children's work

This child's painting was accompanied by a rhyme:
Hurray! All their troubles are gone!
The ice is cleared, the bar undone,
the goblins their mischief cease
to frolic and romp with ease.
Shoo, shoo, sad thoughts, off you run!
Now let's happy be and have fun!

Hurray! Hurray! Hurray!

Work is fun!

This picture by Józef Kowner and the one on page 22 are examples of 18 pictures drawn for an album showing the work done by children in the Lodz ghetto. Each picture had a rhyme like the one on the previous page.

Many of them are very interesting, even if we don't remember they were painted in the ghetto. But many of them also show us the harshness of life there – some artists were determined to leave a record of their people's sufferings. Many artists died because they disobeyed the Nazis' rules about what they were allowed to draw and paint.

As the war went on, the demand for labour in the Lodz ghetto increased and children were put to work. About 700 children were educated as they worked in the underwear and dress workshop. Children also enjoyed the plays and puppet shows that were performed for them in the ghetto.

Art in the ghettos

Several internationally known Jewish artists were confined to the ghettos. Many of them were deliberately sent to the Terezín ghetto, near Prague. There they were encouraged to paint because Terezín was the centre of a huge Nazi **propaganda** exercise. Hitler made a film of this ghetto to try to show the rest of the world that he was providing a good life for the Jews (*see page 44*).

In the years since the war, paintings and drawings have provided us with images of day-to-day life in the ghettos. Some of these pictures appear on these pages.

Ghetto lullabies

Of all the poetry of the ghettos, the lullabies are the most deeply moving. Their words speak to babies and small children of their parents' hopes, fears and despair. This is a lullaby from the Lodz ghetto by Yeshayahu Szpigel:

> *Close your eyes,*
> *And the birds will come*
> *To circle around your cradle.*
> *Bundle in hand,*
> *Our house, ashes and brand,*
> *We're leaving, my child, to seek happiness.*
>
> *God has closed down the world,*
> *And all around us is night*
> *It awaits us with shuddering and fear*
> *We both stand here,*
> *In this hard, hard hour,*
> *And the path leads who knows where.*
>
> *We were chased from our home*
> *Stripped to the bone,*
> *Through the dark, driven into the field,*
> *And hail, snow and wind*
> *Accompanied you, my child,*
> *Accompanied you into the abyss of a world.*

Ghetto diaries

Many people in the ghettos wrote diaries. It is clear from their content that these were written deliberately to keep a record for future generations. The writers went to a great deal of trouble to hide their diaries in places where they would not only be safe from discovery by their guards but also where they would be preserved from damage, if necessary, for some time. People have continued to find diaries since the end of the war, some hidden away or buried in ceramic jars or in specially sealed containers.

The diaries are valuable because they tell us in detail about day-to-day life in the ghettos. They describe the hardships and the struggle of the inmates to come to terms with the cold, hunger and sickness. They record moments of happiness, as well as sadness. They show how much people clung to the hope that everything would one day be back to normal. Some are diaries written by men who were forced to make decisions about the fate of fellow Jews. Sometimes, it is clear that the pain and suffering was so great that there were almost no words to describe them.

One subject that seems to come up in nearly all the diaries is the deportations. Thousands of people from the ghettos were regularly loaded into wagons and taken away. They were often the elderly and small children. Those left behind in the ghettos were deliberately not told where their friends and relatives were being taken. Rumours spread wildly, but slowly the truth began to dawn. People realized that their fellow inmates were never coming back. The constant threat of deportations created a permanent sense of fear and apprehension.

A paper record

The diaries were written either in exercise books or often in the margins of books that had been taken into the ghetto amongst personal belongings.

Extracts from a ghetto diary

16 October 1942

'The word in the street is that the "Liar" [code name for the radio] announced that only 300,000 of the 3,000,000 Polish Jews remain, and that the rest were killed in his deportations. I do not believe it, although one could believe it after watching the deportation procedure. They went out and searched only for people who were unable to work: children under the age of ten, old people over sixty years of age, the ill ... They sent away children up to age ten without parents, sent sick people from the hospitals with the one nightshirt that they'd slept in. For what? It's been said that they took them to Chelmno ... where there's a gas house where they are poisoned ...'

3 August 1944 [the end of the Lodz ghetto]

'I write these lines in a terrible state of mind – we have all of us to leave this ghetto within a few days ... Biebow, the German Ghetto-Chief, held a speech for the Jews ... He asked the crowd if they are ready to work faithfully for the Reich, and all answered "Yes". What sort of people are these Germans, that they managed to transform us into such low, crawling creatures; is life really so worthy?

When I look on my little sister, my heart is melting. Hasn't the child suffered her share? ... What will they do with our sick? with our old? with our young? ... I don't even know if I shall be allowed to be together with my sister. I cannot write more. I am more resigned terribly and black spirited.'

From the diary of Menachem Oppenheim, who was in the Lodz ghetto.

Guards at the gate

In this photograph, German and Jewish police guard one of the entrances to the Lodz ghetto. A crowd of Jewish residents has gathered in the background.

The Kovno ghetto

The Nazis thought that people would never know how they treated the victims of the Holocaust. However, Dr Elkhanan Elkes, who the Germans placed in charge of the Kovno ghetto, ordered that all its inhabitants should help keep a detailed history of the ghetto. They could take photographs, write diaries or poetry and do paintings. The response was enthusiastic. Young and old kept detailed diaries. A keen photographer, George Kadish, took many photographs at great risk to himself. Artists, such as Esther Lurie and Josef Schlesinger, drew and painted pictures. Much of this evidence was lost, but some survived because it was carefully buried or hidden. Some of these works were saved by survivors. Others lay undiscovered for many years after the war. Together, these works make sure that the memories of the appalling conditions and Nazi atrocities in the Kovno ghetto have survived for posterity.

Josef Schlesinger

Josef Schlesinger began his training at the Prague Academy of Fine Arts just before the Germans **occupied** Czechoslovakia. He went to Kovno to join his father and was confined in the ghetto after the Nazi invasion of Lithuania. There he worked in the ghetto's Paint and Sign Workshop. Here, under cover of his work, he organized secret art exhibitions. His pen and ink drawing of a particularly significant event in the ghetto – the public hanging of Nahum Meck in 1942 – was placed in the secret exhibition. Meck had been caught smuggling and had shot at a German guard. Diary entries and children's drawings show that his execution had shocked the inmates. Afterwards, Meck's mother and sister were taken to the square in Fort IX and murdered by the Nazis.

The Hanging of Meck

The Hanging of Meck, Josef Schlesinger, 1942.

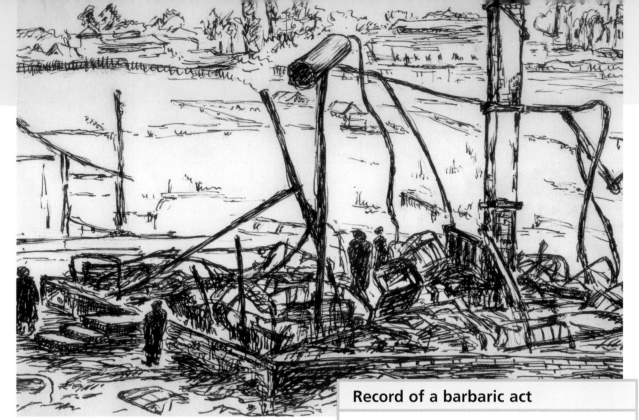

Esther Lurie

The Nazis in the Kovno ghetto also made use of established artists. They were ordered to paint landscapes and portraits. Sometimes they copied great masterpieces. But behind the scenes, they painted what they saw around them. Esther Lurie became very important in creating Kovno's secret **archive**. She had formal training in art and had already won prizes for her work in Tel Aviv (now in Israel), where she designed theatre sets. Unluckily, she returned to Europe late in 1938 and so was caught by the Nazis. Some of her paintings of simple landscapes actually show where dreadful atrocities took place. One area was Fort IX where brutal mass-killings regularly took place. One of the worst of these was on 29 October 1941, when 9200 inhabitants were taken to the square in the middle of the fort and murdered – 4200 of these were children.

Record of a barbaric act

What Was Left of the Hospital, Esther Lurie, (undated) shows the aftermath of the burning of a hospital in the Kovno ghetto.

One of Esther's pen and ink drawings records a barbaric act that happened in October 1941. It shows the charred remains of one of the ghetto's hospitals. There was an outbreak of contagious disease so Nazi officials ordered that the hospital should be burned. Orders forbade any attempt to put out the blaze. All the doctors, nurses and patients, including many children, perished in the blaze. The event is also recorded in surviving diaries. People also feared that any future outbreak would be dealt with in the same way.

Altogether, Esther Lurie produced over 200 paintings and drawings in the ghetto, but many of these were lost. Esther survived and was able to reconstruct some of her lost paintings from photographs of the originals taken at the time.

Records of resistance

Art, music and writing record people's resistance to **Nazi persecution**. There was also more violent resistance in the **ghettos**. Kovno had its own underground organization linked to Jewish **partisans** living in the forests around the ghetto. Many of these had escaped. Other ghettos also had underground organizations that planned armed uprisings. In 1943, rumours of **deportations** sparked an uprising in the Bialystok ghetto in north-eastern Poland. The same rumours were to blame for a larger uprising in the Warsaw ghetto. This began on 18 January 1943 and lasted until 16 May. It was a particularly violent uprising, partly because Jewish resistance fighters, led by Mordecai Anielewicz, openly fought the Germans. A careful record was kept of the events in diaries. These were found hidden in a milk churn after the end of the war.

The Warsaw ghetto's secret archive

In the Warsaw ghetto, historian Emanuel Ringelblum encouraged artists and writers to build up a secret **archive**. It was called *Oneg Shabbat* ('Joy of the Sabbath'). Abraham Lewin was an important contributor and kept a detailed account of the last days of the ghetto. The earliest surviving entry was for March 1942. Despite personal tragedies, he carefully recorded the terror and destruction, until 16 January 1943, when he and his daughter were probably killed. Ringelblum was also executed shortly afterwards. Lewin's diaries were part of the hidden archive, discovered after the war ended.

Inside the Warsaw ghetto

A painting by Roman Kramsztyk, *Old Jew with Children*. This was done in the Warsaw ghetto. The artist was eventually killed by the Nazis in 1942.

Self Portrait

Self Portrait by Gela Seksztajn, who lived and painted in the Warsaw ghetto. She died in Treblinka in August 1942.

From the diary of Abraham Lewin

Wednesday, 22 July 1942
'A day of turmoil, chaos and fear: the news about the expulsion of Jews is spreading like lightning through the town. Jewish Warsaw has suddenly died, the shops are closed. Jews run by, in confusion, terrified. The Jewish streets are an appalling sight – the gloom is indescribable. There are dead bodies in several places ... Beggar children are being rounded up into wagons.'

Friday, 31 July 1942
'The tenth day of the slaughter that has no parallel in our history ... They are driving the old people from the old people's home at 52 Nowolopki Street. Those rounded up are divided up into those fit for work, those able to survive and those not fit to be transported. The last group is killed on the spot.'

Wednesday, 5 August 1942
'The "action" continues unabated. We have no more strength to suffer. There are many murders. They kill the sick who don't go down to the courtyards ... Whoever falls into the hands of the Germans or the Jewish police is seized.'

Sunday, 9 August 1942
'The 19th day of the "action" of which human history has not seen the like. From yesterday the expulsion took on the character of a pogrom, or a simple massacre. They roam through the streets and murder people in their dozens, in their hundreds. Today, they are pulling endless wagons full of corpses – uncovered – through the streets.'

Friday, 21 August 1942
'Yesterday evening after six the Jewish police moved into the buildings which were supposed to have been evacuated by their occupants. They drove the occupants out by force, broke into locked flats, robbed and looted and smashed whatever they found and at the same time seized women, especially those who had no papers. Where did the Jews get this brutality from?'

Jewish partisans and their music

Resistance in the ghettos was doomed to failure, as the destruction of the Warsaw ghetto shows. Whenever possible, young men and women escaped from the ghettos to join partisan groups in the forests of Poland, Ukraine and parts of the Soviet Union. This was dangerous. They not only risked being caught, but they were also frequently rejected by the non-Jewish partisans on whom they depended for shelter and support. The situation seemed to improve from the summer of 1942, as they came to be more accepted. Family camps were established in the forests for Jewish partisans and their families, but only a small number of Jews escaped death by joining the partisans.

By this time, Jewish people were resisting the Germans by actively fighting, derailing enemy trains and blowing up bridges. From 1943, Jewish-only partisan units were formed. These were important because they helped their members to hang on to their cultural identity and the idea of belonging to one nation. Much of this happened during evening sessions around the campfire. Songs were sung to the music of the accordion, often in **Yiddish**. Sometimes, the entertainment was provided by former professional entertainers, such as a group called *Gop so smykom* ('Jump for Joy'), which performed popular songs and dances in the forest camps.

Jewish partisans

This picture shows members of a Jewish partisan unit in Byelorussia during the Second World War.

30

Shmerke Kaczerginski

Shmerke Kaczerginski was a poet and songwriter before the war. He lived in Vilna where he wrote songs about the struggle of the working classes. When he was imprisoned in the Vilna ghetto he continued to write songs about the Jewish struggle. His songs were very popular with the Jewish partisans. He also collected songs and poems from the ghettos to make sure that they were not forgotten. One of these was a song by Hirsh Glik, who had been inspired by the Warsaw ghetto resistance. It became the anthem of the Jewish partisans. Glik was later killed escaping from a labour camp in Estonia. He had been sent there for attempting to organize an uprising in the Vilna ghetto.

Kaczerginski later described how Hirsh Glik had inspired him when they met in the Vilna ghetto. Glik had spent some time in Warsaw and experienced the spirit of those leading the resistance to the Nazis there:

'The next day, Hirsh stopped by quite early. "Listen closely," he said. He sang quietly at first, but with fiery passion. His eyes were ablaze. I wondered: Where does he find such unshakeable faith? As his voice grew firmer, he began to hammer out the words, stamping his feet as if he were now on the march ... "Wonderful, Hirsh, wonderful." Through his words, I felt the impact that the Warsaw rising had made on him.'

The Jewish Partisans' Anthem by Hirsh Glik

Never say that you have reached the final road
Though lead-grey clouds conceal blue
*   skies above,*
The hour that we've longed for now
*   draws near,*
Our steps proclaim like drumbeats:
*   We Are Here!*

From green, palmy lands and countries
*   white with snow,*
We come with all our suffering and woe;
And wherever any of our blood is shed,
Our courage and our valour rise again!

Tomorrow's sun will turn this day to gold,
And this dark night will vanish with the foe,
But should tomorrow's sun await the dawn
*   too long,*
Let this song ring out for ages yet to come!

Not with lead was this song written, but
*   with blood;*
It wasn't warbled in the forest by a bird!
But a people, trapped between collapsing walls,
With weapons held in hand – they sang
*   this song!*

So, never say that you have reached the
*   final road,*
Though lead-grey clouds conceal blue
*   skies above,*
The hour that we've longed for now
*   draws near,*
Our steps proclaim like drumbeats:
*   We Are Here!*

31

Camps and death camps

As soon as Hitler came to power in 1933, he established **concentration camps** in Germany. Anyone who opposed the **Nazis**, or, later, who was thought racially **inferior**, was sent there. From 1942, the Nazis carried out their '**Final Solution**' – the complete extermination of the **Jews** and other **undesirables**. This mass murder was carried out mainly in six **death camps** – Auschwitz-Birkenau, Belzec, Sobibor, Treblinka, Chelmno and Majdanek.

Many were sterilized so that they could not have children. Others were used for medical experimentation or were murdered. This policy spread across German-occupied Europe after 1939. Black prisoners of war were treated very badly in concentration camps such as Dachau and Buchenwald. Black **civilians** in Nazi Europe were put into **internment camps**. Some of these people were artists and musicians.

African Germans

Hitler regarded black people as an inferior race. A number of people of African origin had arrived in Germany at the end of the First World War. They had formed relationships with German women. The children of these mixed relationships were called mulattos. The Nazis hated them in the same way that they hated the Jews.

Josef Nassy

Josef Nassy was an African American living in Belgium. He also had a Jewish background. He was one of 2000 American passport holders who were imprisoned in an internment camp during the war. Nassy was at Laufen. Prisoners at Laufen were kept under the terms of the Geneva Convention (an international agreement protecting foreign prisoners from mistreatment). Josef was allowed to paint. During his three-year imprisonment, he produced over 200 paintings of life in Laufen.

Laufen

Josef Nassy spent the war in this camp at Laufen in Germany. As they were held under the terms of the Geneva Convention, the inmates did not have to wear prison clothes or work. However, the conditions were still bleak, as Nassy has shown.

Concentration camps

At concentration camps such as Dachau and Buchenwald, life was very different. Starvation and severe punishments were routine. The inmates were forced to do very heavy work to help the German war effort. They were literally worked to death.

Besides political prisoners, **Jehovah's Witnesses**, **homosexuals** and Jews, there were thousands of **Gypsies**. They were brutally treated but struggled to maintain their family and cultural life in the camps. Gypsy bands played their traditional music with violins and accordions, often under orders from the guards to 'welcome' prisoners back from a day of hard labour or to drown the sounds of their fellow prisoners being beaten. From 1942, Gypsies were **transported** to the death camps for extermination.

Dachau song

This song of the forced labour gangs at Dachau gives a vivid picture of life there:

Charged with death, high tension wire
Rings around our world a chain.
Pitiless a sky sends fire,
Biting frost and drenching rain.

Far from us is lust for living,
Far our women, our town,
When we mutely march to toiling
Thousands into morning's dawn.
(Refrain)
But we all learned the motto of Dachau to heed
And became as hardened as stone
Stay humane, Dachau mate,
Be a man, Dachau mate,
And work as hard as you can, Dachau mate,
For work leads to freedom alone!

Faced by ever threatening rifles,
We exist by night and day,
Life itself this hell-hole stifles
Worse than any words can say.

Days and weeks we leave unnumbered
Some forget the count of years
And their spirit is encumbered
With their faces scarred by fears.
(Refrain)
Lift the stone and drag the wagon
Shun no burden and no chore
Who you were in days long bygone
Here you are not any more.

Slab the earth and bury depthless
All the pity you can feel,
And within your own sweat, hapless
You convert to stone and steel.
(Refrain)
Once will sound the siren's wailing
Summons to the last role call
Outside then we will be hailing
Dachau mates uniting all.

Freedom brightly will be shining,
For the hard-forged brotherhood
And the work we are designing
Our work it will be good.

Auschwitz-Birkenau

The largest proportion of men, women and children who arrived at Auschwitz-Birkenau after 1942 went immediately to the **gas chambers**. Those who escaped this fate were spared to work. Many children, especially twins, were selected for medical experimentation by Joseph Mengele. For some time, Gypsies were also used for experiments until Hitler decided that they, too, should be killed like the Jews. Others who were useful to the Nazis in the camp in a variety of ways lived longer. These included artists and musicians. You have already read about Dinah Gottlieb (*see page 13*) and David Olère (*see page 5*) whose skills as artists were exploited in Auschwitz. Musicians were also given more privileges than their fellow inmates.

Dinah Gottlieb and the Gypsies

Dinah Gottlieb survived because Josef Mengele admired her work. At the time, the 13,000 Gypsies in Auschwitz were kept in a separate area of the camp. The Nazis had not yet decided whether they were an inferior race and should be killed. Mengele was studying them to identify their racial origins. Dinah was told to draw them because the photographs that had been taken of them were not clear enough for him to study their features in detail. She selected a group of Gypsies as her models. One of them was a young woman called Celine. She was Dinah's age and they became friends. Dinah deliberately painted her portrait very slowly, but once Mengele had all the detail he needed he declared that it was finished. She never saw Celine again. By this time, Hitler had decided on the fate of the Gypsies at Auschwitz. It was extermination. They all died in the gas chambers in August 1944. Dinah survived and went to live in Paris, then later, in California.

Gypsy caravan

This gypsy caravan and violin are on permanent display at the United States Holocaust Memorial Museum in Washington DC. They are a reminder that Jews were not the only victims of the Holocaust.

Fania Fenelon and Anita Lasker-Wallfisch

Fania Fenelon and Anita Lasker-Wallfisch were members of camp orchestras. When they arrived they were treated the same as everybody else – their heads were shaved and a number was tattooed on their arms. Anita tells of how she was questioned about her work before the war. When she said that she played the cello, she was separated from the rest. The conductor of the camp orchestra was the niece of the German composer Gustav Mahler. She took Anita into the orchestra. The orchestra was ordered to play as the forced labour parties were marched out of the camp each morning.

Fania Fenelon was a member of a women's orchestra in Auschwitz. She played for the camp commandant, Josef Kramer, but was also expected to play happy tunes as men, women and children were forced into the gas chambers. Both Fania and Anita survived.

Sunday concert

This photograph shows an Auschwitz Orchestra Sunday concert performed for **SS** officers at the camp.

Excerpt from *Gypsy Song* by David Beigelman

David Beigelman was a professional composer and musician in Poland before the war. He was sent to the Lodz **ghetto** where he was the musical director for the ghetto theatre. He later died in Auschwitz.

> *The night is dark,*
> *as dark as ink.*
> *With quaking heart*
> *I think and think.*
> *No others live in*
> *such grief as we're given*
> *We go unfed:*
> *no crust of bread.*

Wall paintings in Auschwitz

At Auschwitz-Birkenau **concentration camp**, some of the most interesting artwork was done by inmates on the walls. The buildings of the camp are still standing, so we can see the artwork today. Dinah Gottlieb, for example, first came to the notice of her Nazi captors after she had decorated the wall of the dormitory for children that had arrived in the camp from the Terezín **ghetto** in Czechoslovakia. The Czech prisoners used art to protect the children as much as possible from the horror of Auschwitz.

Dinah painted the story of *Snow White and the Seven Dwarfs* at the children's request. Later they performed the story.

Other wall decorations for children that can still be seen show us the skill of the artists. They also show how the inmates tried to bring beauty, dignity and colour into their lives. Stencil paintings of camels and pyramids decorate one of the barrack blocks. Cherubs, horseback riders and kittens add some kind of normality to the washrooms in another block.

Boy on a hobby horse

Adults painted pictures, like this one, on the walls of camp buildings used by children to try to make the surroundings more attractive and colourful.

The *Königsgraben* painting

At Birkenau there was a special penal company (the *Strafkompanie*). This was made up of prisoners the Nazis thought were particularly dangerous because they belonged to the camp's underground resistance movement. Others were sent there as punishment for disobeying camp rules. From May 1942 until July 1943, they were housed in a separate barrack and set to work building the *Königsgraben* (King's canal). This was extremely gruelling work, digging a drainage ditch in a swampy area of Birkenau. The prisoners were given little food and punishments were very severe. Large numbers of prisoners died. An unknown artist painted this scene of their labour on the ceiling of the barracks, where it can still be seen.

Reflection

The end of the war and the defeat of Germany in 1945 brought freedom – of a kind. As survivors emerged shocked and starved from the **concentration camps** and **ghettos**, their ordeal was still not over. They were homeless and penniless. They were still treated badly by their neighbours when they returned to their homes. Hundreds were also to find that they were almost completely alone in the world. To the agonizing memories of their own suffering was added the pain of discovering that their loved ones were lost forever. Many were so distressed and disturbed that it was years before they could talk about their experiences.

For the soldiers, journalists and other **civilians** who liberated the camps, the horror of what they discovered deeply affected them. The images of death, destruction and suffering would never leave them. The reality of the Holocaust was so overwhelming that they too found they could not talk about it. Many turned to art, music and poetry as a way of expressing things. For survivors, it was a means of expressing their anger, their indignation and their deep sense of loss.

Mervyn Peake

Mervyn was born in China in 1911 and returned home to England as a boy. As a young man, he gained a reputation as a painter and illustrator, then as a poet and novelist. When war broke out he went into the army. Towards the end of the war, after leaving the army, he was sent with a journalist to draw the scenes of devastation caused by the war. As a result, he was one of the first Britons to enter the concentration camp at Bergen-Belsen. This experience deeply influenced his work from that time onwards. He was also a writer and he became obsessed with the idea of the struggle against overwhelming power and destructive forces. He expressed this idea in his books, the *Gormenghast Trilogy*, especially in *Titus Alone*. The first book in the trilogy was published in 1946 and the last in 1959.

Witness of death

Gassing by David Olère. After being freed from Auschwitz, David was able to empty out on to his canvas the terrible scenes of the gas chambers that he held inside his head. His collection of paintings is entitled *The Eyes of a Witness*.

The Consumptive, Belsen 1945

Mervyn Peake went into Bergen-Belsen with British troops in 1945. He wrote this poem and made this drawing after he had witnessed scenes of sickness and suffering there:

If seeing her an hour before her last
Weak cough into all blackness I could yet
Be held by chalk-white walls, and by the great
Ash coloured bed,
And the pillows hardly creased
By the tapping of her little cough-jerked head –
If such can be a painter's ecstasy,
(Her limbs like pipes, her head a china skull)
Then where is mercy?

Music of remembrance

The aftermath of the Holocaust also inspired composers. Survivors composed some of the most moving pieces of music, using music to express their deep pain and sorrow. One such piece is called *Terezín*. It was written by a survivor of the ghetto, Karl Berman.

Other works are dedicated to those whose sufferings have become well known, for example Oskar Morawetz's *From the Diary of Anne Frank: Oratorio for Voice and Orchestra*. This is dedicated to Anne Frank and includes parts of her diary set to music. In 1947, Arnold Schoenberg, whose music had been banned by the **Nazis**, wrote *A Survivor From Warsaw*. This is a short but powerful piece based on the story of a survivor of the Warsaw ghetto. It describes the moment when the crowds showed their defiance when faced with death by singing a traditional Jewish song, *Shema Israel* ('Hear, O Israel'). The words are from the Old Testament of the Bible.

In 1962, Russian composer Dmitri Shostakovich composed *Babi Yar* to commemorate the slaughter of 70,000 Ukrainian Jews at a ravine on the outskirts of Kiev. This work, inspired by the Holocaust, is important because it is the first statement against **anti-Semitism** in the history of Russian music. In 1968, the American composer Charles Davidson set many of the poems of the children of Terezín to music. This song cycle is called *I Never Saw Another Butterfly*.

Words of remembrance

It took years for many of the survivors of the Holocaust to speak out about their experiences. At the trial of Adolf Eichmann, who sent thousands of Hungarian Jews to the **gas chambers**, many survivors gave evidence about the terrible things they had seen and endured. Since the trial, the **archives** of oral and written evidence of the Holocaust have grown into a lasting memorial. Artists and writers continue to be drawn to the subject.

Nelly Sachs

Nelly was born in Berlin in 1891. She began writing romantic poems at the age of seventeen. Her first book, a collection of historical tales, was published in 1921. However, the Holocaust changed her work dramatically. Her friendship with a Swedish writer saved her life, as she and her mother were able to leave Nazi Germany. During the war, her poetry became dominated by the cruelty and atrocities experienced by Jews. Her first two volumes of these poems were published in 1947 and 1949. Her work throughout her life continued to reflect her obsession with the suffering of the Holocaust. She received the Nobel Prize for Literature in 1966 and died in Sweden in 1970.

Elie Wiesel

Elie Wiesel was Hungarian. The Wiesel family was taken to Auschwitz in 1942. His mother and younger sister died immediately in the gas chambers.

If Only I Knew by Nelly Sachs

*If only I knew
On what your last look rested.
Was it a stone that had drunk
So many last looks that they fell
Blindly upon its blindness?*

*Or was it earth,
Enough to fill a shoe,
And black already
With so much parting
And with so much killing?*

*Or was it your last road
That brought you a farewell from all
　the roads
You had walked?*

*A puddle, a bit of shining metal,
Perhaps the buckle of an enemy's belt,
Or some small augury
Of heaven?*

*Or did this earth,
Which lets no one depart unloved,
Send you a bird-sign through the air,
Reminding your soul that it quivered
In torment of its burnt body.*

Elie, his father and two older sisters were selected for work. He and his father were sent to Buchenwald, where his father died. After he was freed, Wiesel became a respected academic. His writing has been completely devoted to making sure people know the truth about the victims of the Holocaust, because he was there and he shared their suffering.

Never Shall I Forget by Elie Wiesel

Never shall I forget that night,
the first night in the camp
which has turned my life into one
*   long night,*
seven times cursed and seven times sealed.

Never shall I forget that smoke,
Never shall I forget the little faces of
*   the children*
whose bodies I saw turned into wreaths
*   of smoke*
beneath a silent blue sky.

Never shall I forget those flames
which consumed my faith for ever.
Never shall I forget that nocturnal silence
which deprived me for all eternity of the
*   desire to live.*

Never shall I forget those moments
which murdered my God and my soul
and turned my dreams to dust.

Never shall I forget these things,
even if I am condemned to live
as long as God Himself.

Never.

Memorials

Some of the artistic work inspired by the Holocaust since 1945 can be seen in memorials. This one in Warsaw was erected in 1948 to commemorate the brave resistance of the inhabitants of the Warsaw ghetto.

Never forget

The Holocaust was a human tragedy on an unimaginable scale. The paintings, diaries, letters and poems that survive from the time are extremely important because they help us to recognize that those who suffered and died were human beings – young and old. They had fears, anxieties and moments of joy, just like us. Their only 'crime' was that their culture or religion made them different.

The Terezín ghetto

The *Theresienstadt* (Terezín) was originally a military fort about 60 kilometres (37 miles) from Prague (now in the Czech Republic). From 1941, Czech **Jews** were forced to leave their homes to live there. Soon, hundreds arrived from all over eastern Europe. The overcrowded conditions were as harsh and cruel as in other **ghettos**. However, Terezín ghetto is remembered for its rich cultural life – the beautiful poetry and painting of its children and the amazing creativity of its artists, composers and musicians. Hitler recognized how this could be used for **propaganda**. He showed Terezín to the world as a model settlement where Jews could live and flourish safe from **persecution**. He even opened it up for **Red Cross** visitors so that they could see for themselves what was happening there.

The creativity of the children of Terezín

About 15,000 children passed through Terezín ghetto between 1941 and 1944, but only about 100 survived the war. Most of them died in Auschwitz. They are remembered by the collection of around 4000 pictures and hundreds of poems that they left behind. Although the children suffered cruelty, disease and starvation, they were sheltered from the reality of their surroundings as much as possible. They were still educated. They were encouraged to write and draw. With the help of Friedl Dicker-Brandeis, an artist, they created a bright and colourful world in their paintings. However, their poems show us a deeper fear and longing. It is very sad for us today to read how they hoped that they would one day return to their homes, towns and villages and be reunited with their families, when we know what really happened.

The Butterfly

The last, the very last,
So richly, brightly, dazzlingly yellow.
Perhaps if the sun's tears would sing
Against a white stone.

Such, such a yellow
Is carried lightly way up high.
It went away I'm sure because it wished to
kiss the world good-bye.

For seven weeks I've lived in here,
Penned up inside this ghetto.
But I have found what I love here,
The dandelions call to me
And the white chestnut branches in
the court.
Only I never saw another butterfly.

That butterfly was the last one.
Butterflies don't live here,
in the ghetto.

This poem was written by Pavel Friedmann, who died in Auschwitz in 1944.

Vedem ('In the Lead')

One group of teenage boys produced a carefully handwritten and amazingly creative secret magazine. It was done without the help of adults in a concealed area in their barracks known to them as the 'Republic of Shkid'. Their magazine contained articles, poems and drawings. When the boys were eventually sent to Auschwitz, the magazine was saved by one of the survivors.

Extract from an article in *Vedem*, Terezín, 1943

In this extract from *Vedem*, Petr Ginz describes his task of bringing food from the kitchens to the hospital:

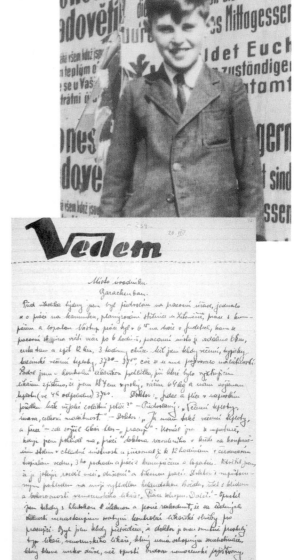

'An Unsuccessful Ramble Through Terezín
At last we set out. The journey was uneventful and we reached the Hamburg barracks, where the dietary kitchen is now situated, without mishap. Recalling my newspaper duties, I tried to get some sort of interview going.
- How many people does this kitchen serve?
- Why do you ask?
- If you want to know, I am the editor of a magazine called *Vedem*.
- That's a good one – an editor – ho, ho, ho. Well, if you must know, about 450. That kind of conversation was not to my taste and so I took the container of mashed potatoes and left ... Oh what pen could describe our sufferings on this arduous pilgrimage! The wind drove sand into our faces, soup spilled from our buckets over our coats and into our shoes... Kališek was pleased. His feet were warm, he said, because hot soup was slushing about in his shoes.'

Music and theatre in Terezín

Between 1941 and 1945, the theatre flourished in Terezín. All sort of plays, cabarets, puppet shows and concerts were performed, all staged with scenery and costumes. This was partly due to the large number of artists and musicians who were sent there. Fourteen operas were performed, including *The Marriage of Figaro, Tosca* and *Cavalleria Rusticana*. This was thanks to the work of Rafael Schechter, a talented pianist and composer. He established a choir in Terezín soon after his arrival in 1941. Schechter and his choir of 150 people were later **transported** to Auschwitz where they died.

Brundibar

This copy of an old photograph shows the final scene from the opera *Brundibar* as it appeared in the propaganda film made by the Nazis in 1944.

Hans Krása and *Brundibar*

Hans Krása was born in Prague in 1899. By the time he was eleven, his first musical composition had been performed in public. He studied music at the German Academy of Music in Prague. He led a fashionable life, mixing with writers, artists and poets. In Terezín he composed several pieces. His best-known work was the children's opera, *Brundibar*, which was not only performed in the ghetto but which was also filmed by the **Nazis** for propaganda purposes. They wanted the world to believe that the inmates were being treated properly.

The opera was first performed on 23 October 1943. It is the story of two needy people who the local children decide to help by holding a street collection. Suddenly, Brundibar, an evil organ grinder appears and takes all the money they have collected. Children played the parts of the birds and animals who make sure that Brundibar returns the money he has stolen. *Brundibar* was performed 55 times. In spite of his talent and success, Hans Krása was sent to Auschwitz where he died in the **gas chambers** on 17 October 1944. He composed what was to be his final work only four days before leaving Terezín.

The puppet theatre

It is amazing that, in spite of living in such awful conditions, people could still make puppets, scenery and lighting effects. Twenty-two puppet shows were performed in Terezín to the delight of the small children in the ghetto.

Victor Ullmann, Petr Kien and the *Emperor of Atlantis*

Victor Ullmann was a student of the composer Arnold Schoenberg in Vienna. He was a totally dedicated and hard-working musician. Like Hans Krása, he composed a huge number of pieces, and continued to write after he had been sent to Terezín. Petr Kien wrote words to go with the music, and, together with Ullman, produced the opera *Emperor of Atlantis*.

In fact, Kien wrote two versions. One was handwritten and the second was typed. The first was fiercely critical of Hitler and the Nazis. The second, much milder version was shown to the camp officials to make sure they would be allowed to perform the opera. On the surface it appears to be a simple story, but the underlying theme is the horror of the **concentration camps**. The main characters are the Emperor, the Loudspeaker, the Drummer-girl and Death. The Emperor is Hitler, the Loudspeaker is Goebbels and the Drummer-girl is Hitler's deputy, Herman Goering. The other characters – the soldier and the young girl – are caught up in the horror of war. In the story, Death goes on strike because he is unable to cope with the devastating effects of war and hunger. Without the help of Death, the Emperor cannot rule. Instead, Death supports the ordinary human beings until the Emperor (Hitler) accepts his own death. This version of the opera was not performed until after the war was over!

Drama

Plays were also performed in Terezín. This was mainly as a result of the work of Gustav Schorsch, who had studied drama in Prague. He was in charge of the theatre section in Terezín. His productions included *Measure for Measure* by William Shakespeare.

The artists of Terezín

The real world of Terezín was captured by a group of talented painters. The Nazis labelled their work 'horror propaganda'. In fact, their paintings portrayed the truth about life in Terezín. The artists were questioned and tortured. Almost all of them died as a result.

Leo Haas

Leo Haas was one of the survivors of the Holocaust. He had studied at the Berlin Art Academy and worked in Vienna before returning to Czechoslovakia. He was deported to Terezín in December 1942. Here, under the cover of working in the Drawing Office of the Technical Department (where artists were used by the Nazis to draw plans for them), he painted and drew the reality of life at Terezín. He was arrested in 1944, imprisoned and later moved to other camps until he was set free at the end of the war. He had a distinguished career after the war, which included being a professor at the Art Academy of Berlin.

Fritz Taussig

Fritz Taussig was known as 'Fritta', the name he used on his paintings. Until 1941, he was a cartoonist and graphic artist in Prague. In Terezín, he was put in charge of the Technical Department and had the job of providing the Germans with drawings and plans. Like Leo Haas, he used his position to do undercover, secret artwork. Unfortunately, in July 1944, some of his work was discovered along with that of others. The artists were sent to Auschwitz. Fritta died there. His wife died in prison in Terezín. Their three-year-old son, Tommy, was adopted by Leo Haas after the war.

Art as a record

Scenes of Life in the Ghetto by Leo Haas is an example of how some artists used art to record what conditions were really like in the ghetto.

TO NENÍ POHÁDKA – TO JE PRAVDA!

Tommy's book

Fritta's son Thomas was the first baby to be born in the ghetto. In fact, Jewish women were not allowed to have babies. If they became pregnant they were given **abortions** free of charge. But it was sometimes possible to hide the babies when they were born. This meant that Tommy's early years were far from those of a normal toddler. In an attempt to make up for this, Fritta produced a very touching book of drawings to celebrate his son's third birthday. The delightful illustrations in the book show Tommy's birthday celebrations as they should have been in a normal world. They are very different to the 'secret drawings' that his father drew of his real surroundings. The birthday album was hidden and discovered after the war. It was later published by the Yad Vashem memorial museum in Israel.

Pavel Fantel

Pavel Fantel was not a professional artist, but he was inspired by the hardships he endured to express himself through art. Pavel was born in Prague. He trained and then became a doctor in the Czech army. He arrived at Terezín in 1942 and worked in the hospital there. During this time, he secretly drew a series of pictures that gave

Real life or a fairy tale?

This picture from Tommy's book shows Tommy running about in a landscape filled with sunshine, butterflies and flowers. The caption reads 'This is not a fairy tale – it's real'.

a cynical view of life at Terezín. In one of these, called *Metamorphosis*, Fantel shows how an inmate of Terezín changed as a result of being imprisoned for four years in the ghetto. It is made up of a series of four pictures. In the first, the man looks plump and well fed. By the time the fourth picture is reached, he is almost a skeleton.

The history of the Terezín ghetto and its prisoners brings home to us very clearly just how much talent was lost by the destruction of life in the Holocaust. It is particularly sad that so many of the talented artists and musicians that were killed were children and young people.

The Terezín diary of Gonda Redlich

Gonda Redlich's diary was discovered in 1967 but only published completely in English in 1992. The original was written in **Hebrew**. It is in two parts. The first is a list of events in Terezín from 1942 until 1944. The second is a diary written for his baby son, Dan, after his birth on 16th March 1944.

Gonda was born in Olmütz, Moravia in 1916. When the Nazis took over Czechoslovakia in 1939, he was studying to be a lawyer. In the ghetto, Redlich was on the committee ordered by the Germans to provide lists of men, women and children to be transported.

At the beginning, no one had any idea what was happening to them. Gonda's diary, however, records his own observations of his surroundings. It talks about his hopes and fears and the awful responsibility of his official position. Occasionally, there is humour. It also confirms the reality of life in Terezín shown, for example, by the artists.

Extracts from Gonda Redlich's diary

January 4–6, 1942
'In the evening, I heard a terrible piece of news. A transport will go from Terezín to Riga (Latvia). We argued for a long while if the time had not yet come to say "enough". Our mood is very bad. We prepared for the transport. We worked practically all night. With Fredy's help, we managed to spare the children from the transport.'

January 8, 1942
'The Germans ordered the construction of gallows. All the people that sent letters are expected to be in grave danger. Haven't we reached the limit? Yet we still argue among ourselves concerning our living quarters. When I think about it, all of this is insignificant compared to the fact that it is possible some Jews may die whose only crime has been the writing of a letter to their relatives.'

January 21, 1942
'Moments of satisfaction. The woman director of the youth office conducted me to a room where they were celebrating the birthday of a small child. The other children sang songs. The sun came out and warmed the room and I almost forgot all the difficulties of our situation.'

A child of the ghetto

Charlotte Buresova's paintings were painted in such a way as to deliberately emphasize the things of beauty amongst the poverty and sorrow of the ghetto.

'Diary of Dan'

On 16 March 1944, Gonda's son, Daniel was born. At this point, he began to write a second diary. This was so that he could keep a record of his son's early years that one day they could look back upon together. The entries in the diary record special moments in Dan's young life and reveal the delight of a father in his baby son:

> March 22nd 1944
> 'After you were born, he (the head of the Jewish community) announced your name: Dan Peter Beck, along with thirty dead and another outbreak of **typhus**. You carried your mother's family name because our marriage was performed in the ghetto and such marriages were not legal according to the law of the land.'

> April 13th 1944
> 'Today we went out with you for the first time. We have a nice baby carriage, a product of the ghetto. Usually the craftsmanship in the ghetto is second rate, but this baby carriage is very pretty ...

> 'Bright afternoons. In the city square, the Jewish orchestra played. A Jewish orchestra, as if a hard war full of blood was not being fought, a war of survival.'

> July 20th 1944
> 'Your eyes are as blue as heaven. This is no poetic exaggeration. Your eyes stand out the most. Everyone praises them ... I wanted to give your mother a gift on her birthday: a picture of you. I asked an artist to draw your picture. Today they arrested the artist, and took him to an unknown place.'

> October 6th 1944 [the last entry]
> 'Tomorrow, we travel my son. We will travel on a transport like thousands before us ... Hopefully, the time of our redemption is near.'

Gonda, his wife and baby did not return from that last journey. They died in Auschwitz-Birkenau.

Timeline

1933

30 January	Hitler and the Nazi Party come to power in Germany
28 February	Decree is signed allowing for the creation of concentration camps to hold political opponents of the Nazis
21 March	Dachau, the first concentration camp, is established
1 April	Campaign to encourage people to boycott Jewish businesses is begun
7 April	Jews employed by the government lose their jobs
10 May	Books classified as 'degenerate' are taken from libraries all over Berlin and publicly burned

1934

5 March	Jewish actors banned from performing
7 June	Jewish students banned from taking examinations

1935

15 September	The Nuremberg Laws remove all rights and freedom from Jews and make them the focus of humiliation and discrimination

1936

A decree is issued that says Jewish doctors and dentists are not allowed to work in state hospitals. Jews cannot become judges, join the military or work in the book trade.

1937

Exhibition of 'Degenerate' Art is held in Munich. This includes works by Van Gogh, Matisse and Cézanne and attracts 2 million visitors.

1938

9 November	*Kristallnacht* (Night of Broken Glass). Jewish synagogues are burned and shop windows smashed. Hundreds of Jewish men are arrested and sent to concentration camps.

1939

1 September	Germany invades Poland
3 September	Second World War begins when Britain and France declare war on Germany

1940

	German and Austrian Jews attempt to find refuge in other countries. The majority are refused entry.
February	First Jews are deported from Germany to ghettos in Poland
30 April	The Lodz ghetto, in Poland, is established.

1941

	The Terezín ghetto is established outside Prague, Czechoslovakia
	The Kovno ghetto, in Lithuania, is established
June	In eastern Europe and the Soviet Union, mobile killing squads begin the mass slaughter of Jews and Gypsies

1942

20 January
The Wannsee Conference, attended by leading Nazis, takes place near Berlin. At this, the 'Final Solution' of the 'Jewish problem' is decided.
The boys of the Terezín ghetto begin producing their secret magazine, *Vedem*.
Gonda Redlich begins writing his diary in the Terezín ghetto

26 March
Deportations to Auschwitz from ghettos and camps in Europe begin

1943

January–May
Resistance in the Warsaw ghetto crushed by SS forces
David Olère deported to Auschwitz
Jewish partisan units formed in the forests of Poland and Lithuania
Children's opera, *Brundibar*, performed in the Terezín ghetto

1944

6 June
D-Day Landings in Normandy, France; the liberation of northern Europe begins
Felix Nussbaum and his family, Gonda Redlich, his wife and baby son Dan, and Petr Ginz all die in Auschwitz

1945

27 January
Soviet forces liberate Auschwitz. David Olère and Dinah Gottlieb are survivors.

11 April
Buchenwald concentration camp is liberated. Elie Weisel is a survivor.

15 April
British forces liberate Bergen-Belsen. Mervyn Peake is among the first Britons to witness the horror of the Holocaust.

7 May
Germany surrenders. The war in Europe is over.
Camps and ghettos such as Lodz, Kovno and Terezín are liberated

20 May
The Nuremberg Trials of Nazi war criminals begin. They last until October 1946.

1947

Arnold Schoenberg composes A *Survivor From Warsaw* in memory of those who died in the heroic resistance to the Nazis
Nelly Sachs' first poetry anthology is published, dedicated to Holocaust victims

1948

14 May
The creation of the Jewish state of Israel is announced. Survivors begin to emigrate there. The Jewish homeland is created at great cost to the Palestinian Arabs who live there. Other survivors seek new lives in places such as the USA, Canada, Britain, Australia and New Zealand.

1962

May
Execution of Adolf Eichmann
Dmitri Shostakovich composes *Babi Yar* in memory of the 70,000 Jews and Gypsies who were slaughtered on the outskirts of Kiev

1968

Charles Davidson sets the poems of the young people of the Terezín ghetto to music, entitled *I Never Saw Another Butterfly*

2000

Britain, the USA and some other countries in Europe observe a national Holocaust Memorial days for the first time. The art, writing and music of those who died and those who survived are moving features in these ceremonies.

Glossary

abortion medical operation carried out to end a pregnancy

anti-Semitism prejudice or hostility towards Jews

archive collection of documents and records

Aryan used by the Nazis to mean people with northern European ancestors, without any ancestors from what they called 'inferior races', such as Poles, Slavs or Jews. Aryans were supposed to be blonde, blue-eyed and sturdy.

boycott refusal to buy goods from a country, an individual or group of people

capitulation surrender, or to give up resisting something

civilian person who is not serving in the military forces of a country

communists people who believe that property should belong to the state and that each person should only be paid what they need

concentration camps camps in which those who were critical of or opposed Nazi rule were imprisoned. *See also* death camps.

crematoria special ovens designed and built to cremate (burn) bodies

death camps prison camps designed for the purpose of carrying out mass executions

degenerate corrupt or immoral

democracy system of government in which a country's citizens vote for their leaders

deportation the selection and transportation of people (deportees) from the ghettos and concentration camps to the death camps for execution

depression economic crisis usually resulting in high unemployment

dictator ruler of a state who takes total power and holds on to it by removing opposition

Einsatzgruppen special mobile forces set up to murder Jews in occupied countries

emaciated thin and weak from hunger

euthanasia programme Nazi programme of 'mercy killing' of the mentally and physically handicapped to preserve the 'purity' of the Aryan race

'Final Solution' term used to describe the plan to systematically wipe out Jews and all racial groups who did not fit into the Nazis' ideal of a pure Aryan race. The plan was discussed at the Wannsee Conference in 1942. It was to be carried out in specially equipped camps using a poisonous gas called Zyklon B.

gas chambers special buildings constructed by the Nazis at concentration camps, in which prisoners were murdered using poisonous gas

ghetto separate part of a city or town, often a slum area, where a minority group of people lived, or were forced to live

Gypsies travelling people who speak the Romany language; the Nazis called any travelling people, or those whose ancestors had been travellers, gypsies

Hebrews Jews who lived in Palestine in ancient times. Hebrew was their language, and a modern version of the language is used in the present-day state of Israel.

homosexual person who is attracted to other people of the same sex

immigration moving from one country to another

inferior not as good as someone or something else

internment camp camp set up to remove from society people whom the government thought to be undesirable

Jehovah's Witnesses a religious group

Jew someone who is a member of the Jewish religion, called 'Judaism'. The Nazis also called people Jews if they had Jewish ancestors, even if they had changed their faith.

Nazi short for *Nationalsozialistische Deutsche Arbeitpartei*: the National Socialist German Workers Party

Nazi Youth organization of young German boys started by the Nazis to make sure that Nazi ideas and beliefs were passed on to young people

occupation when one country invades and rules over another country

partisans resistance fighters in occupied countries who used techniques such as ambushes to drive the Germans out of their country

persecution being treated very badly over a period of time

pogrom organized persecution of a group whose culture and religion are different

propaganda clever advertising or public speeches and displays that have the power to influence the way people think. Joseph Goebbels was Hitler's Minister for Propaganda from 1933 to 1945.

prosperity the wealth or good fortune necessary to live a comfortable life

Red Cross non-political international organization set up to provide assistance to victims of war and natural disasters

Reichstag German parliament

Slavs groups of people native to parts of Russia, Poland and the former Czechoslovakia

Sonderkommandos special groups of prisoners in the death camps, many of them Jews, who took the bodies from the gas chambers to the crematoria

SS short for '*Schutzstaffel*' – security staff. The SS began as Hitler's personal guard. Later, some ran concentration camps and death camps. All the SS swore loyalty to Hitler personally, not to Germany.

transportations the transportations (also known as transports or deportations) were the huge convoys of several thousand people taken from the ghettos and concentration camps to the death camps, such as Auschwitz

typhus an infectious disease

undesirables people in Nazi Germany (and other parts of Europe after 1939) that the Nazis believed to be racially inferior

visa pass or certificate allowing a person to enter a foreign country

Yiddish language spoken by Jews in central and eastern Europe. It is a mixture of German dialect containing Hebrew words and those of other modern languages.

Further reading

Auschwitz, Jane Shuter (Heinemann Library, 1999)
Diary of a Young Girl, Anne Frank (Penguin, 1997)
I Never Saw Another Butterfly: Children's Drawings and Poems from Terezín Concentration Camp, 1942–1944, edited by Hana Volavkova (Schocken Books, 1993)
Ten Thousand Children: True Stories Told by Children Who Escaped the Holocaust on the Kindertransport, Anne L. Fox and Eva Abraham-Podietz (Behrman House, 1997)
The Beautiful Days of My Youth, Ana Novac (Henry Holt, 1992)
The Cap, or The Price of a Life, Roman Frister (Weidenfeld & Nicolson, 1999)
The Past is Myself, Christabel Bielenberg (Chatto and Windus, 1984)

Sources

The author and Publishers gratefully acknowledge the publications from which written sources in the book are drawn. In some cases the wording or sentence structure has been simplified to make the material appropriate for a school readership.

A Cup of Tears, Robert and Michael Lewin (Blackwell Publishers, 1989) p. 29
Anne Frank's Diary (Guild Publishing, 1980) p. 16
Art from the Ashes: A Holocaust Anthology, edited by Lawrence L. Langer (Oxford University Press, 1995) pp. 29, 40
Dachau Song (reproduced courtesy of the US Holocaust Memorial Museum) p. 33
Holocaust Poetry, compiled by Hilda Schiff (St Martin's Press, 1996) pp. 15, 41
I Have Not Seen a Butterfly Around Here: Children's Drawings and Poems from Terezín (Jewish Museum Prague) p. 42
O' The Chimneys, Nelly Sachs (Translation copyright © 1967, renewed 1995 by Farrar, Straus and Giroux, Inc. 'If Only I Knew' reprinted by permission of Farrar, Straus and Giroux, LLC) p. 40
Rise Up and Fight (a CD produced by the US Holocaust Memorial Museum, Washington DC, USA) p. 31
The Glassblowers, Mervyn Peake (Eyre & Spottiswoode, 1950. 'The Consumptive' reproduced courtesy of Methuen) p. 39
The Holocaust Exhibition website of the Imperial War Museum (http://www.iwm.org.uk/lambeth/holoc-ex1.htm) p. 39
The Last Ghetto, edited by Michel Unger (Yad Vashem Publications) pp. 22, 23
The Last Lullaby: Poetry from the Holocaust, translated by Aaron Kramer (Syracuse University Press, 1999) pp. 19, 21, 35
The Terezín Diary of Gonda Redlich, edited by Saul S. Friedman (University of Kentucky Press, 1999) pp. 48–49
Voyage of the St Louis, an online exhibition by the US Holocaust Memorial Museum (http://www.ushmm.com/stlouis/) p. 17
We Are Children Just the Same: Vedem, the Secret Magazine by the Boys of Terezín, edited by Marie Rut Krizkova (Jewish Publication Society, 1995) p. 43

Places of interest and websites

Museums and exhibitions
Imperial War Museum
Lambeth Road, London SE16 6HZ
Tel: 020 7416 5320
Website: *http://www.iwm.org.uk*
The Imperial War Museum in London now has a permanent Holocaust exhibition.

London Jewish Museum
Raymond Burton House, 129–131 Albert Street, London NW1 7NB
Tel: 020 7284 1997
Website: *http://www.jewishmuseum.org.uk*

Or:

The Sternberg Centre, 80 East End Road, London N3 2SY
Tel: 020 8349 1143
The London Jewish Museum regularly features exhibitions and talks about the Holocaust.

Sydney Jewish Museum
146 Darlinghurst Road, Darlinghurst, NSW 2010
Tel: (02) 9360 7999
Website: *http://www.sydneyjewishmuseum.com.au*
The Sydney Jewish Museum contains a permanent Holocaust exhibition, using survivors of the Holocaust as guides.

Websites
Before consulting any websites you need to know:

1 Almost all Holocaust websites have been designed for adult users. They can contain horrifying and upsetting information and pictures.
2 Some people wish to minimize the Holocaust, or even deny that it happened at all. Some of their websites pretend to be delivering unbiased facts and information. To be sure of getting accurate information it is always better to use an officially recognized site such as the ones listed below.

www.ushmm.org
This is the US Holocaust Memorial Museum site.

www.iwm.org.uk
The Imperial War Museum site. You can access Holocaust material from the main page.

www.holocaust-history.org
This is the Holocaust History Project site.

www.auschwitz.dk
The Holocaust: Crimes, Heroes and Villains site.

http://motlc.wiesenthal.com
The Museum of Tolerance's Multimedia Learning Centre site.

Index

SCISSORS,

PAPER,

CRAFT

30 PRETTY PROJECTS ALL CUT, FOLDED AND CRAFTED FROM PAPER

Christine Leech

Quadrille
PUBLISHING

Photography by Keiko O

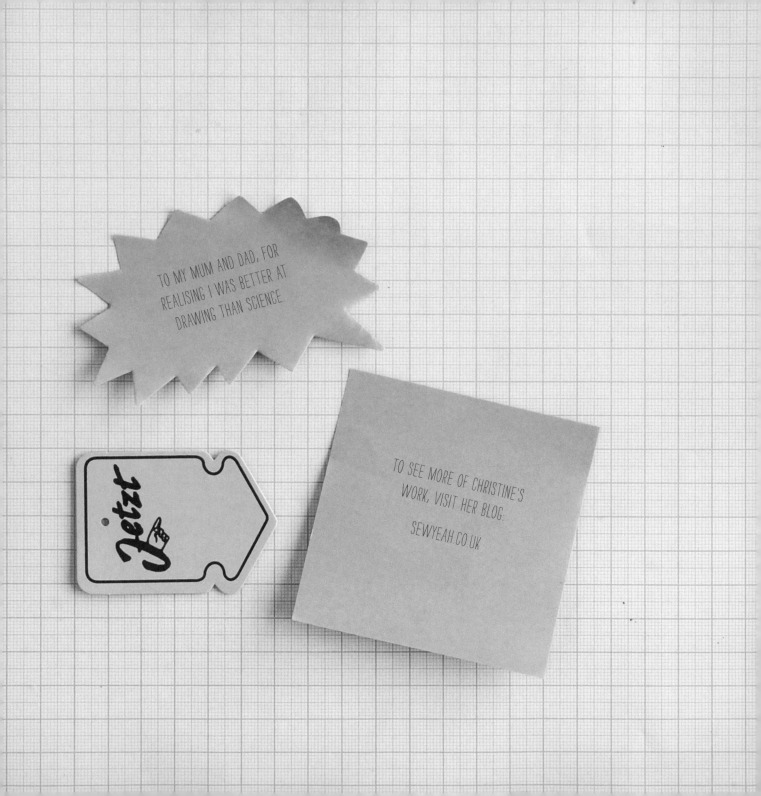

WHAT'S INSIDE?

CONTENTS

INTRODUCTION

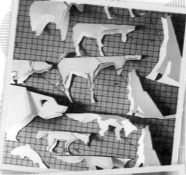

I was so excited to be asked to do a papercraft book as paper is one of my favourite mediums to work in. My training as a graphic designer and illustrator gave me many excuses to play with paper: making giant collages from the teeniest scraps, bending and scoring card into elaborate models and sewing folded sheets into useful sketchbooks. The Rococo Mirror Frame on pages 98–101 is an updated version of some picture frames depicting architectural styles that I made for my Art Foundation course when I was 18, and I used to sell mini notebooks like those on pages 38–41 at the school craft fair.

It's not just plain paper that I love. One of my favourite aromas is the smell of a freshly printed book and, more often than not, I sniff the pages before looking at what's printed on them (you do get some odd looks in bookshops). I also love collecting printed paraphernalia, from vintage bus tickets through German sausage packaging to American shop signage. My collection mostly sits in a box waiting for me to do something with it, but a few bits are scattered through this book and I'm glad to have found a use for them.

There's been a real boom in papercraft in recent years, with scrapbooking and card-making becoming many crafters' passions. The rise of these crafts has led to a miraculous increase in the type of papers, glues, decorations and cutters you can buy, but this book only requires a few basic tools and a simple range of papers. There's a little something for everyone: if you are looking for unusual decorations for your party, make one or all of the various garlands in the book or try the Giant Gift Rosettes on pages 102–105. These would look brilliant at a baby shower or as a wedding backdrop and, speaking of weddings, the bouquet of crepe-paper anemones and camellias on pages 46–49 will last as long as your memories of the day.

I was on a ranch in the US when I was commissioned to write this book and the Colorado Critters on pages 14–17 were inspired by the wildlife I saw while there (though I only got first-hand experience of the deer and bison), as were the Feather Mobile on pages 86–89 and the Lifesize Cardboard Deer on pages 84–85.

Whatever you choose to make, have fun, enjoy it – and mind your fingers!

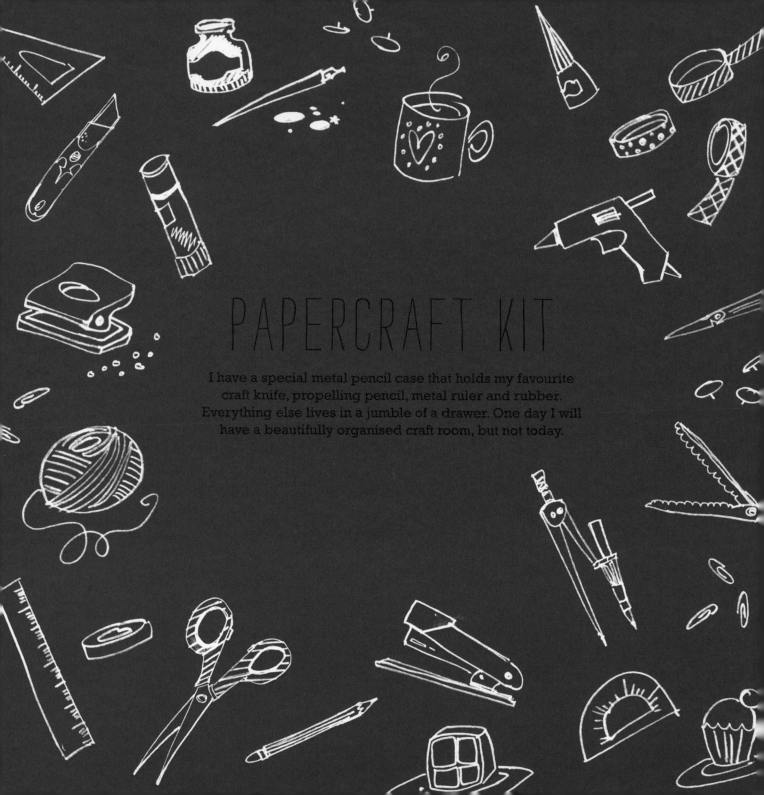

PAPERCRAFT KIT

I have a special metal pencil case that holds my favourite
craft knife, propelling pencil, metal ruler and rubber.
Everything else lives in a jumble of a drawer. One day I will
have a beautifully organised craft room, but not today.

CUTTING THINGS

SCISSORS A variety of scissors will help you with your paper projects. You need large, sharp scissors that can cut through several sheets at a time, small scissors for delicate patterns, and a selection of pinking shears and decorative-edged scissors for ornate work. Don't muddle your fabric-cutting scissors up with your paper-cutting ones. No good will come of it: your fabric scissors will go blunt from cutting paper and your paper scissors will not cut a nice straight edge of fabric.

KNIVES At college all our knives were surgical scalpels with 10A blades, and this is still the type I prefer. These days you can get many different knives, some with retractable, snap-off blades and some shaped like a pen so they are comfortable to hold. Find the knife you are most comfortable with and practise cutting straight lines and curves. ALWAYS cut on a cutting mat, not on your dining table. A utility, or Stanley, knife is good for cutting less fiddly patterns as well as for cutting through thicker card and paper.

CUTTING MAT As I said, always use a cutting mat when using a knife. It provides a safe non-slip surface for your paper and is often made from self-healing plastic, so you can use it over and over again. Most mats have measurements marked out on them, which is handy. If the thing you are cutting is too big for a mat, then please make sure you have something underneath it that you don't mind getting scored.

PUNCHES From the simple office hole punch to the elaborate embossing and shaped punches, there are many different ways to cut paper shapes. In this book I have tried to limit the number of types of punches used, but if you have a hole punch, a 5cm diameter circle punch, and an 8cm- and a 5cm-diameter flower-shaped punch, then you'll have everything you need. But don't worry if you don't have the shaped punches: you can cut the flower shapes with scissors – it will just take a bit longer.

FIXING THINGS

STAPLER The projects in this book only require a simple stapler. I've always fancied one of those long-reach ones that can staple right into the middle of a book, but I haven't really got a use for it. A small stapler with little staples is also useful for tiny corners where a larger stapler may not fit.

SPRAY ADHESIVE Glue in a can. Brilliant. Spray adhesive is great for covering areas of paper with a thin, even layer of glue. It can be permanent or repositionable. When spraying glue, always spray in a well-ventilated space and hold the can at least 20cm from your paper. Move the can quickly and evenly across the area. If you are spraying thin paper, be careful not to spray for too long in one spot as the glue may seep through to the other side. When fixing paper shapes to a backing card, spray the back of the paper shapes not the card as some glues don't dry and you will be left with a sticky mess.

GLUE STICKS Good old glue sticks – one of the least messy forms of glue application. They are great for sticking paper and if you buy an extra-strength type, it is perfect for card, too. You can buy glue sticks that go on coloured and dry clear, which is useful if you only want to cover a particular area of paper as you can see what you're doing.

PVA GLUE PVA (which, fact fans, stands for Poly Vinyl Acetate) is also known as white glue or wood glue. It is very strong, waterproof and dries clear. Great for sticking large areas of card and paper, it can be spread thinly with a spatula or small piece of card, and can also be watered down to make a more malleable, slower-drying glue that is useful for bookbinding. Dried PVA also peels off your hands like old skin.

GLUE DOTS Recently there has been a whole raft of new glue products that have made papercrafting much easier and less messy. Glue dots are one of these inventions. They come on a roll or on sheets in several different sizes. Choose from flat or raised dots, which give your work a nice three-dimensional quality.

GLUE SHEETS Glue sheets are a good substitute for spray adhesive if you just want to cover a small area. Basically, they are glue-covered sheets and when you place your paper onto the glue, the glue transfers to your paper and gives it an adhesive back.

GLUE GUN Glue gun = fun. Hot glue guns and cold glue guns both melt glue sticks to give a quick-drying liquid adhesive that is great for sticking card and decorations. The hot glue guns just melt the glue at a higher temperature and hotter glue burns more, so take care.

MASKING TAPE This beige papery tape is easy to tear, remove and reposition. It has a little bit of stretch in it, which is useful when making card hinges.

DOUBLE-SIDED TAPE I love double-sided tape. It is super-sticky but not messy and it fixes things instantly. Available in narrow or wide rolls, the narrow kind is the one I prefer. When I use the wide sort, I always find myself having to cut narrow strips from it!

WASHI TAPE A genius tape, with all the prettiness of beautiful Japanese rice papers, but with the sticking qualities of masking tape. Perfect for wrapping presents and fixing pictures to walls when you want something prettier than boring old Sellotape or pins.

GAFFER TAPE A strong, extremely sticky, cotton-based tape that tears easily when you have the knack – which I don't! Good for sticking large pieces of cardboard together.

MEASURING THINGS

RULERS
When using a craft knife or scalpel, a metal ruler is a must. I have countless plastic rulers with nicks in them where the knife has veered dangerously and annoyingly into the ruler. It's useful to have both a 1m metal ruler – useful for measuring and cutting long, straight lengths – and a shorter metal ruler for the smaller projects. A small metal ruler is also good for making really crisp folds in paper. Just run the end of the ruler along the fold.

GEOMETRY SET
A basic geometry set of compass, protractor and right-angle set square will come in useful for many different things. If you can find a large right-angle set square, buy it as it will be invaluable when it comes to cutting squares.

DRAWING THINGS

DIP PEN AND INK
Though a little messy (which is part of their charm), dip pens and Indian ink create a beautiful decorative effect. Alternatively, you can get many types of felt-tip pen with different nibs that give a variety of calligraphic and artistic lines.

PROPELLING PENCIL
Clicky pencils are great; there is no need for pencil sharpeners as you'll always have a sharp point. But the thin lead of a propelling pencil gives you much more accurate measuring points.

ERASER
Though a sparkly strawberry-scented eraser might look (and smell) good, a simple white rubber eraser is preferable for removing unwanted pencil lines. Always clean your eraser on a spare piece of paper before you use it on your project.

OTHER THINGS

BRADAWL
This tool, which is more often found in your toolbox, is good for making holes through card or through multiple sheets of paper. Always use it on top of an old piece of wood so you don't damage your table.

SPLIT PINS
You can get lots of decorative split pins these days, so there's no need to use only the round, gold-coloured ones. Craft shops sell packs in various colours and shapes. They are good for making hinges and for joining several pieces of paper together.

DECORATIVE BITS AND BOBS
Sequins, small buttons, adhesive gemstones and glitter are all great for making your paper projects a little bit more special.

NEEDLES, THREADS AND SEWING MACHINE
Several projects in the book use a needle and thread, either to join pieces of paper together or to hang the final project. A variety of needle sizes will be useful and a sewing machine wouldn't go amiss either.

PAPER FACTS

There are lots of types of paper in the world and I like them all, whether it's the edible rice paper stuck on the bottom of a coconut macaroon or the giant, endless rolls of paper I see when I'm visiting a printing press.

PAPER WEIGHTS

Paper comes in three main weights, classed loosely as light, medium and heavy. The weight is measured in gsm, or grams per square metre. This is literally how many grams a square metre of paper would weigh – not that you often see a square metre of paper!

And then there's card. Some papers can be called lightweight card and a lot of card could be called heavyweight paper, but you get the drift…

If you hold a piece of paper between your thumb and forefinger and it droops, it's classified as lightweight; if there's a slight sag, then it's medium-weight and if you can balance your cup of tea on it, then it's card. *

LIGHTWEIGHT PAPER - 35-90 GSM
Tissue paper, newsprint, origami paper, photocopy and printer paper

MEDIUM-WEIGHT PAPER - 105-165 GSM
General letter paper, brown paper, pastel paper

HEAVYWEIGHT PAPER - 175-335 GSM
Postcards, business cards, watercolour paper, posh invites

CARD - 400 GSM+
Mount board, grey card

PAPER SIZES

Paper sizes are most commonly expressed with an A rating, from the giant poster-sized A1 to the tiny business card A8. Any sheet of A-size paper can be folded to produce a sheet with another A measurement. The most common size is A4, which is two A5s or half an A3.

PAPER TYPES

Different papers are good for different things. I've used a variety of papers in this book. Here are some of my favourites.

TISSUE PAPER Often found wrapped around a pretty present, tissue paper is one of the thinnest papers you can find.

CREPE PAPER Crepe paper is perfect for making paper flowers as its stretch and strength allow you to curl petals and twist stems. Try to buy florist's crepe paper as it is much more durable than many art-shop versions. (See the Anemone and Camellia Bouquet, pages 46–49.)

TRANSLUCENT PAPER Not just the grey tracing paper of your school days. Now you can get see-through paper in a myriad of colours. Stronger than tissue paper, it is useful for stained-glass effects and for layering up different colours.

PRINTER PAPER Easy to come by and in loads of colours, printer paper is good for practising on when trying out a project for the first time. I made prototypes of most of the projects in this book from white A4 printer paper first.

ORIGAMI PAPER There are lots of different types of origami paper, ranging from traditional handmade and gilded to slick and shiny with modern designs. One- or two-sided, origami paper folds beautifully and has many uses beyond its traditional, historic one.

BROWN PAPER One of my favourite papers. I love the subtle lines embossed on it and its cheapness! Used in the right way it doesn't look cheap at all. (See the Rococo Mirror Frame, page 98–101.)

PASTEL PAPER Many projects in this book use Murano pastel paper. It folds beautifully, comes in a brilliant range of colours, is nicely textured and ink doesn't bleed on it, so you can draw nice crisp lines on it. (See the Colorado Critters, pages 14–17.)

HANDMADE PAPER Handmade paper is especially beautiful as each sheet is unique. From paper that includes flower petals or sequins, to embossed, gold-leafed, hand-cut and dyed, there are a million handmade papers to choose from. As the paper is made by hand, the fibres are not as 'organised' as in machine-made paper. This means it may not fold or tear as neatly as its factory-made counterpart.

WATERCOLOUR PAPER This comes in several weights and has either a smooth or a rough texture. Some have a pretty deckled (feathered) edge that is the result of the manufacturing process.

CORRUGATED CARD I'm not sure what corrugated card's real use is, but I think it's probably for packaging things to protect them. It doesn't just come in brown rolls and sheets, though. You can get it in many colours. (See the Rustic Quilled Decorations, pages 90–93.)

WALLPAPER Wallpaper offcuts or samples are brilliant for projects that need either a more robust paper or long strips. The often oversized prints make it perfect for larger-scale projects. (See the Giant Gift Rosettes, pages 102–105.)

MOUNT BOARD Mount board is a nice sturdy card often used, as the name suggests, for mounting work, be it your still-life exam pieces or your holiday snaps. It comes in A1 sheets and smaller. Always buy the largest sheet you can as it is better value. If you're not keen on carting large sheets around with you when out shopping or on the train home, some art shops will help you cut it down to a more manageable size. It is best cut with a craft or utility knife. (See the Pigeon Post, pages 22–25.)

GREY BOARD This sad-looking board, often made from recycled fibres, is strong and perfect for bookbinding and for making boxes and folders. It comes in thicknesses ranging from 1mm to 3mm.

WORKING WITH PAPER

You don't need many supplies or specialist knowledge to make a successful paper project, but here are some tips for getting the best results.

PORTRAIT VERSUS LANDSCAPE

These are quite obvious terms for the way a paper rectangle is orientated. Paper that is wider than it is tall is landscape; if it is taller than it is wide, then it is portrait.

MAKING TEMPLATES

There are many templates at the back of this book and I recommend making card templates from them. They will last longer and are easier to draw and cut around. If you have a computer and printer, you could scan the templates, enlarge them to the size you want on a photocopier, then print them in a pale colour or at 20% of black onto your chosen paper. If you trace the templates from the book, instead of then transferring the template to the paper, tape it and the paper to your cutting mat and cut out both at once. This way you won't have pencil lines that will need rubbing out later.

PAPER GRAIN

Paper is made from fibres that are pulped together with water and dyes, then pressed and rolled flat. During this process, the fibres mostly lie down in one direction, which creates the grain of the paper. When you roll a piece of paper into a tube, you will be able to roll it more easily one way than the other. The easy way follows the way the grain is running. It is useful to know this as paper folds much more easily with the grain than against it. In bookbinding, make all your pages with the grain running parallel to the binding of the book; that way the pages won't become wavy.

ROLLING PAPER

If you are working on a project that requires tubes or cones (see the Colorado Critters, pages 14–17), then it helps if you warm up the paper first to relax the fibres in the grain. Start by finding the grain of the paper and roll a loose tube with the grain. Roll this tube back and forth on a table or between your hands for a while, then try to roll a tighter tube or cone. This way you will get a better effect and fewer creases in the paper.

If you have a large roll of paper that you want to lie flat, roll it out then roll it back on itself the other way. This encourages the fibres to lie flat. Ironing paper also helps but be careful, as heat can wrinkle some printed papers. Iron your chosen paper under a sheet of newsprint to protect your paper as well as the iron.

TEARING PAPER

Paper tears differently according to the grain and also according to the way you tear it. It tears much more easily and produces a straighter line if you tear with the grain rather than against it.

You also get different effects according to the way you hold and pull the paper. Imagine holding a portrait piece of paper in both hands. If you move your right hand towards you and your left away from you, you will get a different effect than if you pulled your left towards you and moved your right hand away. This is useful to know when deciding on the finish of tear you want on particular projects.

FOLDING PAPER

Again, paper folds better when working with the grain than against it, though this is less noticeable when using with lightweight papers.

To help fold heavier-weight papers, you can score along the foldline (see scoring paper, below) or fold against the edge of a ruler.

Many origami folds have special names. The most common ones used in this book are mountain fold and valley fold. Again, these are quite obvious terms – a mountain fold looks like a mountain and a valley one… yup, that's right.

To make your fold crisp, pinch it between your fingers and run your nails along it or place the paper on a flat surface and run the edge of a metal ruler or special folding tool along it.

SCORING PAPER

Scoring paper helps make folds crisper and neater and also helps you bend and fold curves inwards. When I score paper I use the back (blunt) side of my craft knife and a metal ruler for straight lines or my free hand for doing curves (A). Don't dig the tip of the knife into the paper as it will drag; just press the long side of the blade firmly into the paper and pull. Be careful if you are scoring very thin paper as you can cut right through it.

Alternatively, you can use the blunt side of a pair of scissors. A dried-up ballpoint pen works well, too – though I always worry that it's going to come back to life and ruin my work. Remember to score on the correct side of the paper depending on whether you need a mountain or a valley fold.

After scoring a curve, pick the paper up and pinch it gently between your fingers to persuade the paper to curve (B).

CUTTING PAPER

Paper can be cut using scissors or a knife. I prefer a knife as the cut is much more accurate. Ideally, if you are working with medium- to heavyweight paper, you should change the blade of your knife for each new project or change it a couple of times while working on the project.

If you are working on a small delicate papercut, it is sometimes easiest to attach the paper (and the template, if using) to the cutting mat with masking tape to secure it.

Always cut the inside lines of the pattern first and the lines of the exterior/outline shape last. And don't try to cut too much of the design in one go. Do little sections at a time and go slowly.

If you're cutting a curvy shape from card or thick paper, cut small sections away rather than trying to cut a big curve in one go.

CURLING PAPER

Several projects call for curled paper. Curl the paper by holding the paper strip in one hand and running a closed pair of scissors along its length. The will paper curl when you reach the end. A firmer pull gives a tighter curl (C and D).

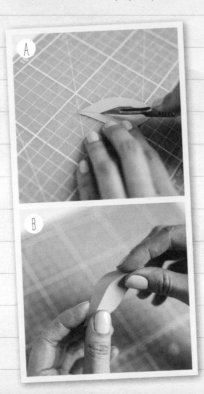

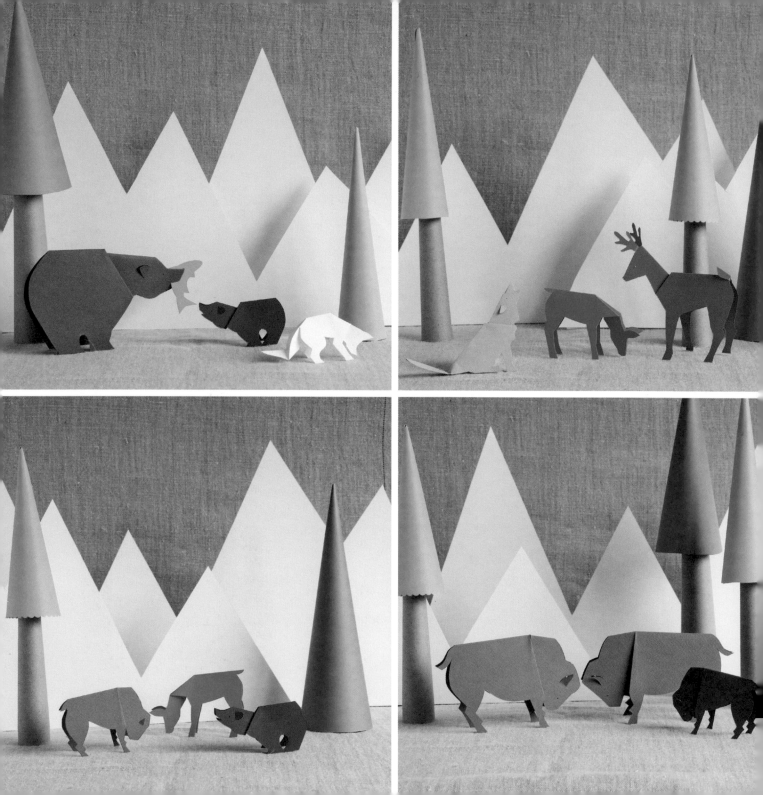

COLORADO CRITTERS

Last summer I holidayed at the beautiful Zapata Ranch in Colorado, USA. These paper animals were inspired by some of the creatures I saw while I was there. To be fair, I didn't actually see a bear or a wolf or a snow fox, but I definitely saw deer!

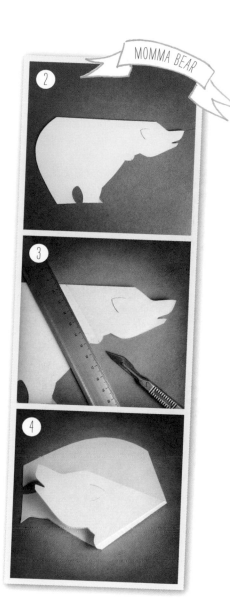

MOMMA BEAR

SUPPLIES

A4 sheets of medium-weight paper in various colours

Pencil

Scissors

Craft knife and cutting mat

Metal ruler

Pin

makes 1

All these critters are made in the same way; the only difference is how you fold their necks and tails.

TO MAKE MOMMA BEAR

1. Fold the A4 piece of card in half lengthways. Using the template on page 115, place the template onto the card with the top edge along the foldline. Using a sharp pencil, trace around the template, making small marks at the bear's neck where the crease lines are indicated.

2. Using scissors, cut out the bear just inside the pencil line. That way there will be fewer pencil marks to rub out later. Using a craft knife, cut out the bear's ears.

3. Using the blunt back edge of the craft knife and a metal ruler, score the two crease lines across the bear's neck.

4. Fold the bear along both the scored lines. Run your fingernails along the scored lines to crease firmly.

CONT. >>>

5. Open out the bear and make an inverse fold on her head at the line marked fold A; push her head down and in-between her front paws.

6. Holding onto the bear's back, just behind fold A, mountain fold her head out from between her paws along fold B so she looks like picture 6B.

7. Using a pin, push in the point to make the bear's eyes.

8. Using the template on page 115, trace and cut out the fish from a different colour card and place in Momma Bear's mouth.

TO MAKE BABBA BEAR

Babba Bear is made in exactly the same way as Momma Bear using the templates from page 115 but, as his neck creases are in slightly different positions, his neck reaches upwards instead of keeping flat.

MOMMA BEAR

TO MAKE MOMMA DEER

1. Follow Momma Bear steps 1–8 using the template on page 114.

2. To make the deer's tail reach upwards, score a line at the point marked fold C then open her body out flat and fold up her tail. Close her body again and her tail will automatically fold over her back. You can also fold her antlers for added character.

3. Don't forget to make her eyes with a pin. Unless, of course, you want to be able to ask… "What do you call a deer with no eyes?" *

TO MAKE BABBA DEER

The Babba Deer template looks slightly odd as her head is upside down, but all will become clear when you fold her neck.

1. Follow Momma Bear steps 1–3 using the template on page 114. Score Babba Deer's neck line and fold her neck flat to one side.

2. Open Babba Deer out then inverse-fold her neck between her front hooves.

3. Fold Babba Deer flat again and her head will be the right way up so she can snuffle around in the grass looking for treats.

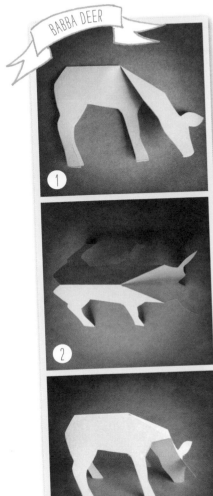

BABBA DEER

1

2

3

TO MAKE SNOW FOX

1. Follow Momma Bear steps 1–3 using the template on page 114.

2. Snow Fox's neck is folded in the same way as Babba Deer's.

3. For his tail, make an inverse fold between his hind legs so his tail points straight down.

4. Next, make a second inverse fold so his tail points out to the side.

TO MAKE WOOLFIE

1. Follow Momma Bear steps 1–3 using the template on page 114.

2. Woolfie's neck is folded in the same way as Babba Bear's.

3. Woolfie's tail is folded in the same way as Momma Deer's. If you prefer the tail not to lay flat, adjust the fold.

TO MAKE THE BISON FAMILY

The Bison Family are made in the exactly the same way as the Bear Family.

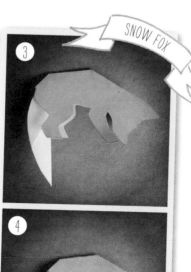

SNOW FOX

3

4

BIRDHOUSE DESK TIDY

A sticky-note dispenser and paperclip holder in the shape of a birdhouse. What more could you want?

SUPPLIES

A3 sheet of 3mm grey card

Craft knife

Metal ruler

Cutting mat

Masking tape

PVA glue

Double-sided tape

Selection of brightly coloured papers in plains or prints (I used origami paper)

Glue stick

Pack of bright pink sticky notes

Circle cutter

makes 1

TO MAKE THE BIRDHOUSE

1. Using the templates on pages 116–117, trace and cut out the birdhouse front and back from the thick grey card. From the same card, cut one 7cm x 6cm rectangle for the base and two 7cm x 5.5cm rectangles for the sides.

2. Cut out the circular entrance on the birdhouse front. The easiest way to do this is to cut lots of straight lines across the circle, all crossing in the middle, then cut away each wedge-shaped segment in turn. (The hole will eventually be covered, so it doesn't need to be super-neat.)

3. Place the two birdhouse sides either side of the base so edges of the same length touch. Use masking tape to join them together. The masking tape will act as a hinge so the sides will be able to fold up. Place the front and back of the birdhouse on the remaining sides of the base and secure with masking tape.

4. Fold up one side and the front of the birdhouse so their edges touch and use masking tape to fix them in place (it's easier to place the masking tape on the outside of the box now).

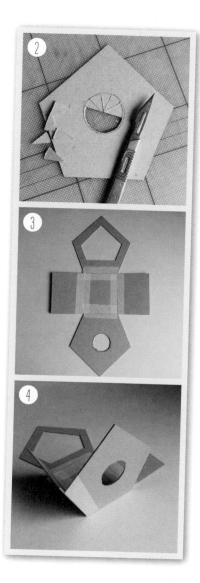

CONT. >>>

〉〉〉

5. Repeat with the other side of the birdhouse and then fold up the back to create a roofless box. To reinforce the birdhouse sides, run a little PVA glue along the inside joints and allow to dry.

TO COVER THE BIRDHOUSE

6. Cover the front of the birdhouse with strips of double-sided tape, then peel away the protective backing. (Double-sided tape fixes the paper firmly in place but also makes the box more rigid. You can use PVA glue but this can get messy and doesn't hold the paper in place instantly.)

7. Place a piece of origami paper right side down on a flat surface, then place the birdhouse, sticky side down, on top. Use scissors to cut away the excess paper, leaving a 1cm border all around.

8. Repeat with the back of the box. To cut the opening, run the craft knife from the corners to the centre of the hole and cut away the excess paper, leaving a 1cm border along each edge. Fold this paper into the hole to create a neat edge. Repeat at the front.

9. Fold the excess paper into the box, creasing or cutting the paper at the corners to make them neater. Use double-sided tape or a glue stick to glue the excess to the inside of the box.

10. Cover the three outer sides of the box with a glue stick. Cut a 7.5 x 21cm rectangle of origami paper. Place it on the box with a 1cm allowance, starting at one side then pressing it onto the glue over the base and up the other side. Try to keep the edges of the paper flush with the front and back of the box. Fold over the two short ends of paper into the box.

TO LINE THE BOX

11. Using the templates again on pages 116–117, cut out the front, back, base and sides from origami paper. Cut away the paper to create the openings on the front and back.

12. Cover the inside of the box with a glue stick, then stick the pieces in place. Start with the front and back, then the base and finally the sides. Press down firmly and allow to dry.

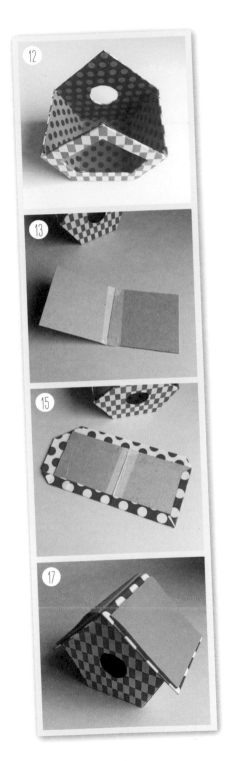

TO MAKE THE ROOF

13. Place the two card roof pieces together so they are almost touching, then join with a strip of masking tape. Run a second piece of masking tape over the other side of the join to reinforce it. The roof must hinge in the centre so it sits neatly on top of the birdhouse.

14. To cover the roof, run a length of double-sided tape all around the rectangle on the upper side of the roof.

15. Place a 10 x 20cm rectangle of origami paper right side down on the table. Place the card, sticky side down, on the origami paper, trimming the paper as shown in the picture to get neat corners. Fold over the edges of the paper and glue in place on the underside.

16. Cut six strips of 5 x 80mm double-sided tape and place them all around the top of the birdhouse along the very edge of the card.

17. Place the roof on top of these strips and press it firmly in place. It's best if there is a slight overhang at the front of the birdhouse and the rear is flush with the back. Split the pad of sticky notes in two and use double-sided tape to fix each half to the roof.

18. Use a circle cutter to make a 'polo mint' from white paper to cover any messy edges around the front entrance. Make the outer hole 40mm and the inner one 25mm. Glue this to the front of the box over the hole.

19. Either hang your birdhouse from a hook on a noticeboard or sit it on your desk. You'll never be at a loss for sticky notes and you'll always have somewhere to store your paperclips and office odds 'n' ends.

PIGEON POST

These natty little pigeons do a great job of keeping all your mail and important bits of paper neat and tidy. Fix them to your wall or noticeboard for an organised life.

SUPPLIES

A5 sheet of coloured mount board

Cutting mat

Craft knife

Selection of coloured pastel papers in 10cm, 8cm and 5cm squares

Dip pen and black ink or black calligraphy pen

Double-sided tape

Scraps of coloured paper for eyes and accessories

Hole punch

makes 1

TOP TIP

If you have only one colour of mount board, using spray adhesive, stick different-coloured paper over the board to create different-coloured birds.

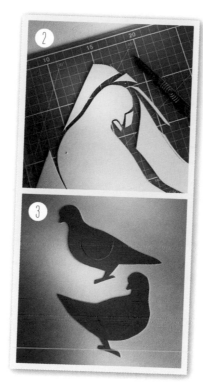

TO MAKE THE PIGEONS

1. Using the templates on pages 116–117, trace the pigeon outlines onto the reverse of the mount board.

2. Lay the mount board on the cutting mat and, using a craft knife, cut out the pigeons. As the pigeons are quite curvy in shape, the easiest way to achieve a neat finish is it to cut away small pieces at a time. Do not try to cut an entire curve in one go.

TO MAKE THE PIGEONS' WINGS

3. Cut the curve of the pigeon's wing slit between marked points A and B.

CONT. >>>

>>>

4. Using the wing templates on page 116, trace the three different-sized wings onto the three different-coloured pastel papers. Using the dip pen and ink or calligraphy pen, draw a curly line to accentuate the scalloped edge of each wing.

5. Once the ink is dry, cut out each wing piece and run a strip of double-sided tape along the top edge on the reverse side.

6. Layer the wing pieces on top of each other to build up the wing. Remove the protective backing from the tape and stick down the small and medium-size wing pieces. Finally, stick the entire wing onto the pigeon body so it covers up the wing slit.

Now accessorise each pigeon in a different way.

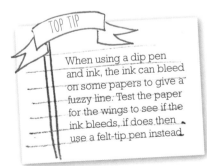

TOP TIP

When using a dip pen and ink, the ink can bleed on some papers to give a fuzzy line. Test the paper for the wings to see if the ink bleeds, if does then use a felt-tip pen instead.

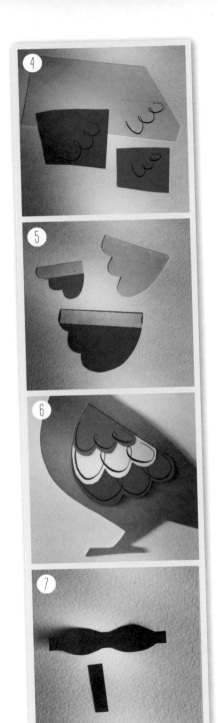

TO MAKE THE BOW TIE

7. To make the bow tie, using the templates on page 116, trace and cut out the two bow tie pieces. Fold the body of the bow tie where indicated then fold the centre of the tie around the body. Fix the tie in place on the reverse with a little double-sided tape. Using the dip pen and ink, draw a bow tie shape onto the paper bow tie.

TO MAKE THE EYES AND OTHER ACCESSORIES

8. Cut out a small oval for each eye and, using a hole punch, create a perfect circle for the pupils.

9. Using a hole punch, make a selection of paper buttons and necklaces. To make the headpiece, follow the instructions for the roses on page 55.

Selection of pieces of patterned wallpaper and coloured paper

Craft knife or scissors

3mm thick grey card in the following sizes:

SMALL BOX

　Four 12cm squares

　One 12 x 11.7cm rectangle

LARGE BOX

　Four 23 x 18cm rectangles

　One 23 x 17.7cm rectangle

RECTANGULAR BOX

　Two 28 x 12cm rectangles

　Two 12 x 12cm squares

　One 28 x 11.7cm rectangle

(You will notice that the base of the box is very slightly smaller than the four sides. This allows the base to fit snugly between the sides.)

LARGE TRIANGLE

　Two 8 x 25cm rectangles

　One 8 x 10cm rectangle

SMALL TRIANGLE

　Two 18 x 13cm rectangles

　One 13cm square

Craft knife

Double-sided tape

Masking tape

Pencil

Glue stick

makes 1 of each

DOLL'S HOUSE STORAGE SYSTEM

Is it a doll's house? Certainly! Is it a church? Could be! Is it a nifty bit of storage for your home office? Oh yeah, it's that too!

TO MAKE THE SMALL BOX

1. Cut a 16cm square of coloured paper. Place it coloured side down on a flat surface. Put the 12 x 11.7cm rectangle of grey card in the middle of the square. Attach lengths of double-sided tape along each edge of the card. Cut away the corners of the paper as shown and remove the tape's protective backing.

2. Fold one edge of the paper over onto the card, tuck in any stray little bits to create a neat corner and press it onto the double-sided tape.

3. Fold the adjacent edge of paper onto the card in the same way. Repeat until all the edges have been folded in and attached.

CONT. >>>

>>>

4. Use masking tape to attach each of the four square grey card sides of the box to the base. Masking tape allows you to reposition the pieces if necessary and it stretches as you fold the sides of the box up.

5. Fold the sides of the box up one by one. As you fold them up, use masking tape to join two adjacent sides together at the corner (5A).

The corners should abut each other, as shown (5B).

6. When you fold up the fourth side, it should fit snugly between the sides of the box and the slightly smaller base.

7. Reinforce all the joins with more masking tape.

TO COVER THE BOX

8. Stand the box in the centre of a piece of patterned wallpaper, print side down, and large enough to cover all sides (approximately 40cm square). Draw around the base of the box with a pencil. Tip the box onto one of its sides and draw around the side. Tip it back to the centre then down onto another side. Repeat until you have a pencilled outline of all four sides and the base. Remove the box.

9. Add a 2cm border at the top of two opposite sides and a 2cm border on three edges of the remaining two opposite sides. Use scissors or a knife to cut out the paper. Trim each corner at an angle as in step 1.

10. Attach lengths of double-sided tape along each of the four edges of the base of the box, then stand the box in the centre of the paper, pressing firmly so it sticks to the paper.

EXTRA!

Instead of using double-sided tape to attach the paper to the box, you could use glue stick or PVA. These do allow for repositioning of the paper but it is more messy!

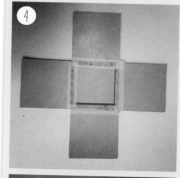

11. To cover the first two opposite sides of the box with paper, tip the box down again onto one of the sides of paper with the three extra flaps (11A). With the box still lying down, attach double-sided tape to the box along the two sides and the inside edge of the open top. Fold the flaps onto the tape and press firmly (11B). Repeat on the opposite side. (To keep the paper nice and flat, it is best to keep the box on the table and roll the two opposite sides down in turn onto the paper. This works better than folding the paper up over the side.)

12. With the box sitting on its base, attach double-sided tape along the edges of one of the uncovered sides, on top of the coloured paper flaps. This time, fold the paper up over the side and press it down to stick it in place. Repeat on the opposite side. Fix the top edges of paper inside the box with double-sided tape.

EXTRA!

Of course you could make a quick version of these boxes simply by covering old shoe or gift boxes, but they might not be as sturdy.

13. To cover the inside of the box, cut four 11.7cm squares from the same paper as you used on the inside base.

14. Cover each of the inside faces of the box with glue stick and glue one of the squares of paper to each face.

15. Make the large and rectangular boxes in the same way. The triangles are made similarly, but it is easiest to make the card triangle first, then cover it with paper and finally cut rectangles of lining paper to cover the inside.

BIRDCAGE POP-UP CARD

13 × 29cm rectangle of medium-weight turquoise paper

Metal ruler

Pencil

Cutting mat

Craft knife

13cm square of medium-weight ivory paper

Spray adhesive

Masking tape (optional)

Glue sheets (optional)

Scraps of plain and patterned coloured papers for the birds and banner

16 × 2cm rectangle of medium-weight pale green paper

Glue stick

Dressmaking pin

Double-sided tape

makes 1

When I was 11, I had a birthday card from my aunt that had a beautiful house on it whose windows and doors all opened. I used it for years after as a kind of Advent calendar countdown for my birthday. This card is a little inspired by that one.

EXTRA!

It's good to use temporary glue when fixing the birds to their hinges, then you can make sure you get them in just the right position before fixing them more securely.

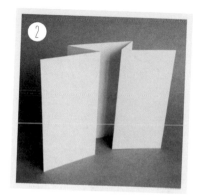

TO MAKE THE BASE CARD

1. Make a small mark at the centre of one long side of the 13 × 29cm rectangle of turquoise paper. Measure and mark 4cm to the right from this centre point, then measure another 4cm to the right and make a third mark. Repeat to the left of the centre mark to make two more marks. Repeat on the opposite long side of the turquoise rectangle.

2. Place the rectangle on the cutting mat and, ignoring the centre mark, use the craft knife and metal ruler to score four straight lines between the marks, then crease the rectangle along the scored lines.

CONT >>>

》》》

3. Copy the template on page 118 and attach it to the ivory paper either with a light spray of spray adhesive or with masking tape around the edges. Cut out the birdcage. (See page 13 for hints on cutting paper.) When cutting the doors, leave the hinge area intact.

4. Cut the birdcage in two down the centre. Score the door hinges so the doors can open and close.

5. Place one half of the birdcage onto the creased turquoise rectangle, making sure that the edge of the birdcage lines up with the crease, as shown. Lift the door and pencil lightly around the 'door frame' onto the green paper below. Repeat with the other half of the birdcage.

6. Cut away the turquoise paper around the 'door frame'. Attach the halves of the birdcage to the front of the turquoise paper using either spray adhesive or glue sheets.

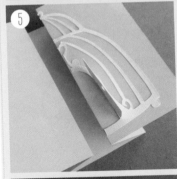

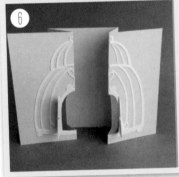

TO MAKE THE BIRDS AND BANNER

7. Using the templates on page 118, cut all the relevant pieces from the plain and patterned papers.

8. To make the banner three-dimensional, score and fold where shown. Fold lines A away from you and lines B towards you.

9. Cut the 16 x 2cm rectangle of turquoise paper in half lengthways. Score four lines each 1cm apart from the next at one end of each of the strips.

10. Use a glue stick to lightly glue Bird 1 to the unscored end of one of 8cm strips so its beak just overlaps the end.

11. Glue the banner onto the strip, under the bird's beak and overlapping its body. Glue the wing to the bird and make an eye with a pin.

12. Place a little double-sided tape or glue onto the first scored square of the strip, then fold it up into a cube and fix it in place, as shown.

13. Glue Bird 2 to the second strip, then repeat step 12 and add a wing and make an eye. Place a

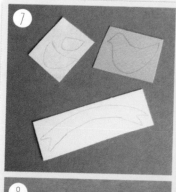

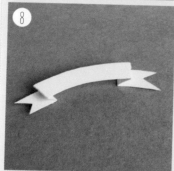

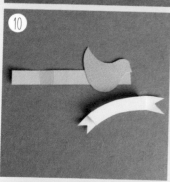

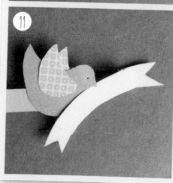

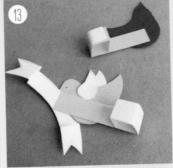

double-sided tape on the back and side of each bird's cube.

14. Remove the protective backing from the double-sided tape and place Bird 1 and its banner on the inside of the card so that one face of the cube is attached to the back of the card and one is attached to the side flap.

15. Repeat with Bird 2, making sure you can see the bird through the door when the card is closed.

16. Using the templates from page 118, cut flowers from patterned papers, then stick to the inside of the card.

BIRD AND NAME GARLAND

This simple little card gives the recipient a lovely surprise when they open it and pull a long string of letters from the envelope.

Pencil

White paper

Scissors

Spray adhesive

One 10cm square of decorative paper per letter

One 10cm square of thin coloured card per letter, plus one for the bird

Masking tape

Cutting mat

Craft knife

Scraps of coloured paper for bunting and bird's wing

Large-eyed needle

Embroidery thread

Glue stick

Large luggage tag

Envelope

1. Start by making the name template. Either write the name freehand on white paper or print out the name using a computer font, making each letter about 10cm tall. You can get lots of free decorative fonts online (see Resources on page 126 for websites). Cut out the name into its individual letters

2. For each letter, use spray adhesive to stick together one square of decorative paper and one square of thin coloured card. Choose attractive combinations of paper and card. Lay the template of one of the letters on top of the doubled-up square. Fix it in place with some masking tape, then attach the two pieces to your cutting mat with masking tape top and bottom.

3. Carefully cut out the letter with a craft knife.

4. Repeat steps 2 and 3 for each letter.

CONT. >>>

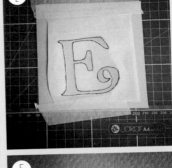

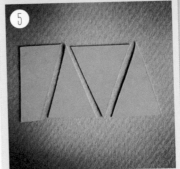

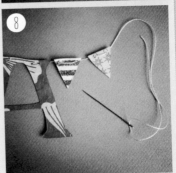

makes 1

>>>

5. To make the bunting, cut three 6cm rectangles from paper or card. Use scissors or a craft knife to cut these into triangles or use the template on page 122.

6. Using the templates on page 122, cut out the bird pieces.

7. Thread a large-eyed needle with embroidery thread long enough to attach the whole name and the bunting. Sew the bird onto the thread through the holes marked on the template, leaving about 10cm of thread for hanging. Cover the thread by gluing the wing over it with glue stick.

8. Sew bunting alternating with letters onto the thread and finish off by tying on the luggage tag.

9. Write your message on the luggage tag, then carefully concertina the garland into an envelope.

EXTRA!

Instead of a name you could spell out congratulations or happy birthday or even the date of a special occasion.

Happy birthday, Lovely

JAPANESE BOUND NOTEBOOKS

These notebooks are made from one large sheet of watercolour paper folded to make the leaves of the book. Their size makes them ideal to carry around with you to use as sketchbooks or to make notes when inspiration strikes.

SUPPLIES

A1 sheet of medium-weight 135 gsm watercolour paper

2 bulldog clips

Right-angle set square

Pencil

Craft knife and cutting mat

Metal ruler

Drill with 2mm drill bit (or bradawl)

Block of old wood, for drilling

Large needle

1m coloured butcher's twine, string or thin ribbon

makes 1

TO MAKE THE BASIC BOOK BLOCK

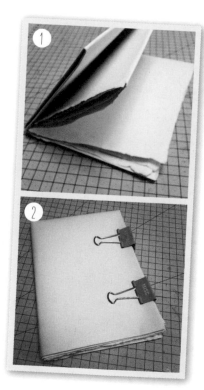

1. Lay the sheet of paper landscape format on a clean, flat surface. Fold the paper into sixteenths, this will take four folds.
Fold 1: fold in half widthways.
Fold 2: fold in half from top to bottom.
Fold 3: fold in half widthways again.
Fold 4: fold in half from top to bottom again. Depending on the thickness of your paper, folds 3 and 4 may prove tough but a good, hard squash will help. You now have your basic book block with a spine and 16 pages, some of which are joined at the folds.

2. Next, you need to release the joined pages. First hold the book closed by placing bulldog clips along the long rough edge opposite the spine.

CONT. >>>

〉〉〉

3. Using the set square placed against the spine, draw a faint pencil line 5mm in from the top edge of the pages. Repeat along the long edge. For the second short edge, measure and mark a line 18cm from the line at the top edge. (You will find it easier if you move the bulldog clips around as you mark the lines.)

4. Using a metal ruler and craft knife, neatly trim the pages along the pencil lines. (Again, move the bulldog clips as you trim each side.) You now have an 18cm tall notebook of 16 pages.

5. Return the bulldog clips to the long edge of the notebook, opposite the spine. Referring to the appropriate guide on pages 118–19, use a metal ruler and pencil to mark the holes where indicated on the guide. Place a block of wood underneath the book block and use a drill and drill bit to make small holes at the marked points.

EXTRA

Decorate the cover of your book with rubber stamps, hand-lettering or pieces of patterned paper. If you want to add a patterned paper cover, wrap a sheet of paper around the book block before step 3, then trim it along with the book pages to the same size before continuing to follow the rest of the instructions.

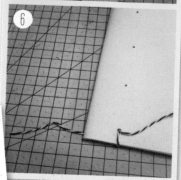

TO MAKE THE BOOK WITH RED BINDING

6. Thread the needle with twine and, starting at the bottom, begin binding the book together as follows:

Enter hole A from the rear of the book. Leaving an 8cm tail end of twine, take the twine around the base of the book and back into hole A from the rear.

Take the twine around the spine of the book and back into hole A from the rear.

Enter hole B from the front, take the twine around the spine and back into hole B from the front.

Enter hole C from the rear, take the twine around the spine and back into hole C from the rear.

Enter hole D from the front, take the twine around the spine and back into hole D from the front.

Enter hole E from the rear, take the twine around the spine and back into hole E from the rear.

Take the twine around the top of the book and back into hole E from the rear.

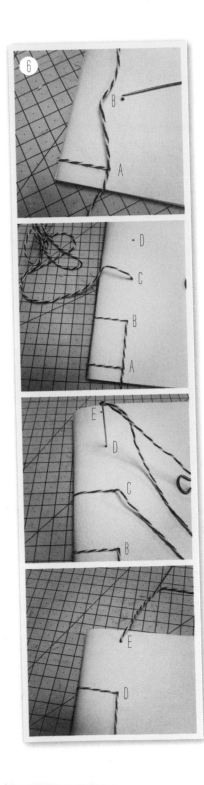

7. Travel back down the book spine, stitching from hole E to D at the front of the book, hole D to C at the back of the book, and hole C to B at the front of the book.

8. To finish off the binding, tie a knot at the rear of the book between holes A and B.

9. When you're confident with this binding, have a go at the brown and the blue books using the stitch guides on pages 118–19.

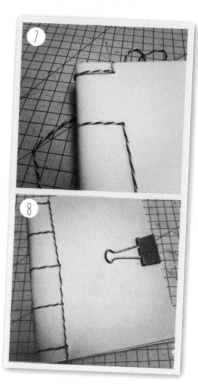

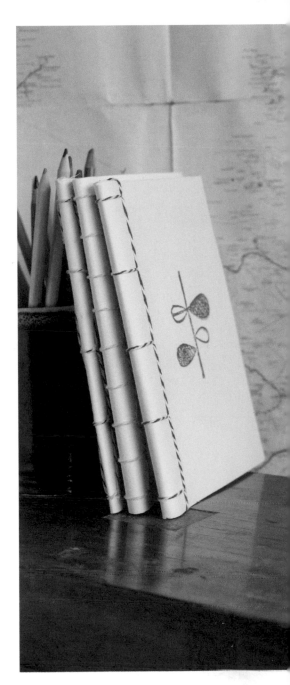

WEDDING GUEST BOOK

SUPPLIES

Two A4 pads (not spiral-bound) of thin watercolour paper backed with thick grey card

Craft knife and cutting mat

Metal ruler

Double-sided tape

2 rectangles of differently patterned handmade paper 3cm larger than A4 all around

Pencil

Masking tape

Glue stick

Decorative-edged scissors

Two A4 sheets of brown paper

Spray adhesive (optional)

Bulldog clip

Two 2cm screw posts

Block of old wood, for drilling

Drill and drill bit the same size as the screw posts

Screwdriver (optional)

PVA glue

Small envelopes

makes 1

I've made several of these for my friends' weddings. A guest book is lovely to give as a gift, but keep it with you throughout the day and get all the guests to sign their name and add a little message. The envelopes dotted throughout the book are good for storing keepsakes and if you can get your hands on an instant camera to add some photos, then that's all the more fun!

TO MAKE THE BOOK'S COVER

1. Separate the pads of watercolour paper from their covers but keep the backing card as these will become the book's front and back covers. Separate the individual sheets of paper. Remove any excess glue from the spine edge of the paper.

2. Place one of the pieces of thick grey card on the cutting mat and use a craft knife and ruler to cut a 5mm strip off one of the short sides. Discard the strip. Measure and cut off a 3cm strip from the same short side so you now have a larger and a smaller piece of card. Attach a strip of 1cm wide double-sided tape along one short side of the larger piece of card and another along one long side of the smaller piece of card. Set these aside.

3. Centre the uncut A4 piece of thick grey card on the wrong side of one of the rectangles of patterned paper.

Draw around the card, then remove. Remove the protective backing from the double-sided tape on the cut pieces of grey card and place the two pieces of card, tape side down, on the drawn rectangle so their short sides butt up to the lines. Having cut away the 5mm strip in step 2, there will be a gap of 5mm between the two pieces of card. This will form the hinge for the front cover of the book.

3

CONT. >>>

4. Cut all four corners of the paper at an angle, leaving approximately 2mm near the corners of the card. Attach strips of double-sided tape along all four sides of the card, right along the edge.

5. Starting at the top, long side of the card, remove the backing from the tape and gently pull the flap of paper down onto it, pressing firmly to make sure it is stuck down all around.

6. Repeat at the adjacent short side. Where the paper overlaps at the corner, tuck the little extra piece of paper into the fold to hide it. Repeat on the two other sides of the card.

TO MAKE THE BOOK'S SPINE

7. Cut a 12 x 25cm rectangle from the other rectangle of patterned paper. Place the rectangle, patterned side down, on a flat surface and run a length of double-sided tape along its long left-hand edge. Lay the front cover of the book on top so the patterned paper overlaps the main part of the cover by 15mm. The spine also reinforces the hinge.

8. Attach a short length of masking tape along the inside edge of the cover and fold the top edge of the spine down onto it (8A). Fold the rest of the top edge of the spine at a slight angle (8B) and cover the remainder of the spine with glue stick. Pull the glued spine onto the cover of the book and press it in place.

9. While the glue is still drying, gently fold the hinge back and forth a couple of times to allow the paper to stretch naturally over the hinged area. Keep pressing the paper flat as you do this and it will settle into place.

10. Repeat steps 4–8 with the other A4 piece of thick grey card to make the back cover.

TO FINISH THE BOOK

11. To hide the raw edges on the inside of the covers, use the decorative-edged scissors to cut 10mm all round off the two A4 sheets of brown paper. Cover the back of each of the pieces of brown paper with glue stick or spray adhesive and press them in place on the inside of the covers.

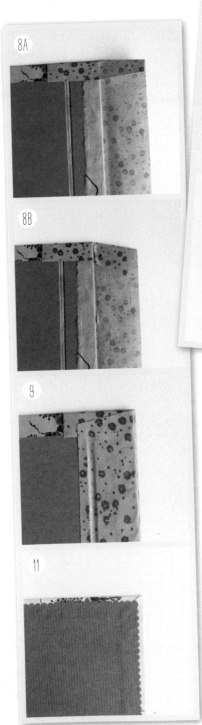

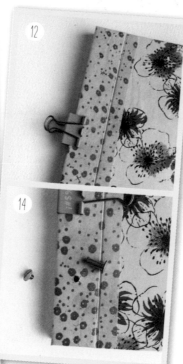

14. Push the long part of a screw post through one of the drilled holes from the front. Screw the short part into the post and tighten with a screwdriver if necessary. Repeat with the other post.

15. Glue pretty envelopes onto pages throughout the book for guests to use to hold their little souvenirs of the day. You can also leave notepaper and luggage tags on tables or by the book so people can write messages to add to the book later.

12. Sandwich the pieces of watercolour paper between the front and back covers and line them up so all the edges are neat. Hold them together with a bulldog clip. Mark the positions of the screw posts on the spine, 15mm in from the edge and 50mm from the top and bottom

13. Place the book on the piece of wood. Using a drill bit to match the diameter of the screw post and holding the book firmly to stop it spinning round with the drill, drill a hole through one of the pencil marks. Repeat for the other pencil marks.

ANEMONE AND CAMELLIA BOUQUET

Nothing quite matches the beauty of real flowers but these paper versions of two of my favourite flowers make a quirky and long-lasting bouquet for any bride. Using a cupcake baking tray ensures the flowers hold their beautiful curved shape.

SUPPLIES

Pencil

Card, for template

Scissors

Florist's crepe paper in white, black and lime green

Cupcake baking tray

PVA glue

Pinking shears

Ten 2cm diameter paper or polystyrene balls

15cm diameter polystyrene ball

Small bowl or mug

Pearl-headed pins

20cm grosgrain ribbon

makes 1

TO MAKE THE ANEMONES

1. Copy the anemone petal template from page 120 onto card.

2. Cut six rectangles of white crepe paper just larger than the template. Layer them on top of each other, making sure the grain of the crepe paper runs from what will be the top of the petal to the bottom. Place the template on top of the pile, draw around it and cut the petals out.

3. Holding both sides of the pile of petals between your thumbs and forefingers, gently pull them apart to make the petals curl.

4. Cut a disc of white crepe paper 2cm in diameter and place it in the bottom of one of the cupcake compartments in the baking tray. Fix three of the petals to the disc with a blob of PVA glue. The petals should overlap.

CONT. >>>

>>>

5. Glue the remaining petals on top of the first three so they all overlap. Finish with a blob of glue ready for the next step.

6. Use pinking shears to cut a disc of black crepe paper 8cm in diameter. Make 2cm snips all around the disc to create the stamens. Glue this in the centre of the white petals.

7. Roll some scraps of black crepe paper into a ball about 2cm in diameter. Cover this with a piece of black crepe paper and smooth it into a pebble shape. Glue it in the centre of the anemone and leave to dry.

TO MAKE THE CAMELLIAS

8. Copy the camellia petal templates on page 120 onto card.

9. Using the templates, cut four small, seven medium and five large petals from white crepe paper.

10. Stretch and curl the petals as before.

11. Cut another disc of white crepe roughly 3cm diameter and place it in the bottom of a cupcake compartment. Glue the five large petals onto the disc so they overlap each other slightly.

12. Glue the seven medium petals onto the large ones, again making sure they all overlap. It's best to do this in two stages: first making a round of four petals, then a round of three.

13. Glue the four small petals in place on top. To make the centre of the camellia, cut a rectangle of white crepe 3 x 15cm and fold it into fifths. Cut a deep arch along one of the short edges of the folded rectangle so when you open it out, you have a scalloped edge.

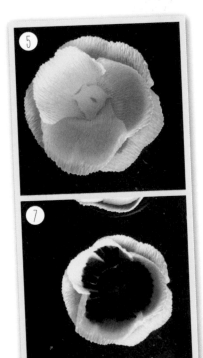

14. Roll the scalloped rectangle into a flower bud shape and glue to the centre of the flower. Allow to dry.

TO MAKE THE BUDS, SMALLER FLOWERS AND LEAVES

15. To make a bud, cover a 2cm diameter paper or polystyrene ball in a piece of white crepe paper. Glue it in place underneath the ball.

16. Cut a 3 x 24cm rectangle of white crepe paper and fold it into eighths. The grain should run sideways.

17. Cut a deep arch along one of the short edges of the folded paper, as before.

18. Open out the scalloped rectangle and fix one end underneath the ball. Gently stretch and wrap the rectangle around the ball, gluing it in place as you go. Allow to dry.

19. To make the smaller flowers, cut scalloped rectangles and roll them up in the same way as you made the camellia centres.

20. Use pinking shears to cut leaf shapes from the lime green crepe paper.

TO MAKE THE BOUQUET

21. Make approximately 16 anemones, 12 camellias, eight buds and some leaves.

22. Cover the 15cm diameter polystyrene ball in white crepe paper and place it in a small bowl or mug so it doesn't roll around.

23. Start pinning the larger flowers into the ball: a couple of pins in each flower should hold it in place. When you are happy with the arrangement, glue the flowers in place more securely. Use the buds and make leaves and smaller flowers to fill any gaps between the large flowers.

24. Fold the ribbon in half and glue and pin it in place at the top of the bouquet so it can hang from the bride's wrist.

EXTRA!

If possible, buy good-quality florist's crepe paper (see Resources on page 126). It has amazing stretch and durability that cheaper papers don't possess.

FLORAL GIFT BOX GARLAND

The uses for these delicate little flowers are endless. Here they are the finishing touches to a beautifully wrapped gift, but they could be used on a greetings card or as place settings. A collection of flowers in the middle of a table would be nice and the teeny tiny ones would be beautiful as confetti.

CONT. >>>

SUPPLIES

Two 8cm squares of coloured paper, for large flowers

Two 5cm squares of coloured paper, for small flowers

4cm squares of coloured paper, for leaves

Scissors

Craft knife and cutting mat

Metal ruler

Bradawl

Small metal split pins

Length of thin ribbon or gold cord (optional)

Gift box

Glue stick or glue dots

makes 1

TO MAKE THE FLOWERS

1. Using the enlarged templates on page 120, trace and cut the petal shapes from coloured paper. You need two petal shapes in different colours for each finished flower.

2. Take one of the petal shapes and, using the blunt back edge of the craft knife, score two straight lines as marked on the template (A and B). Turn the shape over and score the two diagonal lines marked in blue (C and D).

3. Fold the petal shape along the line marked A. Open it out and fold again along the line marked B, then turn it over and fold along the lines marked C and D.

>>>

4. Working around the shape, pinch each quarter together to give a slightly three-dimensional effect.

5. Repeat steps 1–4 with another piece of paper in a different colour.

6. Using a bradawl and resting on a piece of wood, make a hole in the centre of each petal shape.

7. Place one petal shape on top of another and push a split pin through the two holes. Arrange the petals so both sets are visible.

8. Repeat steps 1–7 until you have made as many flowers as you like.

TO MAKE THE LEAVES

9. Using the enlarged template on page 120, trace and cut out the leaf shapes from coloured paper. Score a line three-quarters of the way down the centre of the leaf and crease.

10. To use the flowers and leaves to decorate a gift box, make holes in the leaves and thread them onto some thin ribbon or gold cord and wrap around the box. Use a small amount of glue or a glue dot to fix the flowers in place on the top of the box.

ROSE GIFT TAG

○ ○ ○ ○ ● ○ ● ○ ● ● ○ ○ ○

These roses are possibly the simplest but most effective paper flowers there are. They can be made tiny or giant, but are beautiful, whatever their size.

SUPPLIES

Selection of squares of coloured paper in various sizes

Scissors

Glue gun

makes 1 per square of paper

EXTRA!

These roses look really cute glued to branches of twisted willow for a springtime table centre.

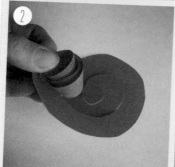

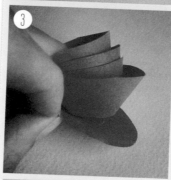

1. Cut a spiral from a square of paper. Make sure the spiral is neither too wide nor too narrow. If you prefer, you can draw the spiral onto the paper before cutting.

2. Starting at the outside edge, roll the spiral up, keeping hold of it to stop it unrolling.

3. When you get to the end of the spiral, use a nice blob of glue from a glue gun on the centre to hold the rose 'petals' in place.

4. Make clusters of roses in different sizes and in a variety of colours to decorate your gifts. Additionally, make a few leaves to accompany the roses following the instructions on page 61.

PASSION FLOWER GIFT TAG

Passion flowers are one of my favourite flowers. Although this is a stylised version of a passion flower, designed to be used as a gift tag, it is just as gorgeous as the real thing.

1. Copy the templates on page 120 onto card and use them to cut out the large flower shape from the purple paper and the small flower shape from the white paper.

2. On one side of the flowers, score along the dotted lines as shown on the template, then flip the flowers over and score along the dashed lines.

3. Work around the flowers, concertinaing the petals as you go. The flowers will begin to close in on themselves. Cut a small hole in the centre of each flower.

4. Roll the rectangle of yellow paper around a pencil, fixing it at one end with a short piece of Sellotape.

5. Remove the pencil and cut the rectangle into several thin strips along its length until you reach the Sellotape. Curl each strip with scissors to make the curly centre of the passion flower.

6. Insert the curly centre into the white flower, then put both inside the purple flower. The Sellotape at the end will act as a stopper.

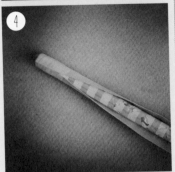

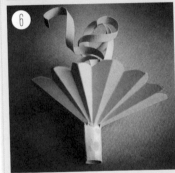

DAISY GIFT TAG

∘ ∘ ∘ ◦ ◦ ● ∘ ◦ ● ● ● ◦ ◦

This clever little flower holds a surprise inside. Open it up and the bloom reveals a hidden message at its centre.

SUPPLIES

20cm square of yellow paper

10cm square of orange paper

8cm square of white paper

6 x 10cm rectangle of green paper

PVA glue

Scissors

Craft knife and cutting mat

Metal ruler

makes 1

1. Using the enlarged templates on page 120, trace and cut out one yellow daisy, one orange base flower and three green leaves from the pieces of card. Gently score along the lines on the daisy shape where indicated.

2. Starting at the top and working all the way round the daisy, fold the petals inwards along the five diagonal scored lines.

3. Pinch each petal together along the six straight scored lines.

4. Starting at one side and working in a clockwise direction, gently press the petals down. They will fall to the side and overlap each other to close up the flower. This may require a little wiggling and gentle persuasion!

5. Open up the flower again and glue the daisy centre in place. Write a message on it, if you so wish. Glue the daisy to the orange base flower.

6. Score and crease each leaf approximately half way along their spines. Glue the leaves between the yellow daisy and the orange base flower.

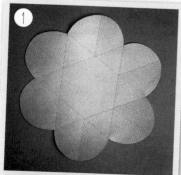

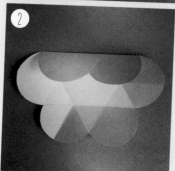

OWL GIFT BOXES

Fill these cute little boxes with sweeties to make great goodie bags for parties. Or they are the perfect size for the safe delivery of baubles, bangles and beads.

SUPPLIES

A4 sheet of light- or medium-weight card

Masking tape

Craft knife and cutting mat

15cm square card in contrasting colour

Double-sided tape

Scissors

Washi tape

makes 1

TO MAKE THE BOX

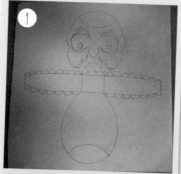

1. Using the enlarged template from page 121, trace the owl gift box onto the A4 sheet of card.

2. Place the card on the cutting mat and stick the edges down with masking tape so the card will not move around when you are cutting.

3. Using the craft knife, cut out the owl's face where marked on the template: cut away his eyes, eyebrows and wings, but only make slits for his beak and tummy feathers.

4. Cut out the rest of the owl, except the teeth on the side flaps – it is easier to do this later.

5. Score where shown on the template – the curve at the top of the owl's head, the curve at the top of his back, the four lines around the base of the box, the four lines along the edges of the side flaps, and the lines for the beak and feathers where indicated.

CONT. >>>

6. Using the enlarged template on page 121, trace and cut out the insert from the 15cm square of card.

7. Fix strips of double-sided tape along both edges of the side flaps. Cut the tape in line with the scored lines as shown so no tape is visible once the box is made up.

8. Cut notches in the edges of the flaps to create 'teeth'. These help the flaps bend in a smooth curve, following the shape of the owl.

9. Fold the flaps up along the scored lines and remove the protective backing from the tape.

10. Lay the owl face down on a clean, flat surface and fold up the base and sides to start forming the box. Press one side flap onto the owl, following his shape. Repeat on the other side.

11. Place a short strip of double-sided tape on the inside of the box behind the owl's face and attach the insert.

12. Fold up the owl's back onto the other edge of the flaps. Press to fix in place.

13. Fold closed the curved flap at the top of his head and the curved flap at the top of his back and fix in place with a piece of washi tape. Your owl is born!

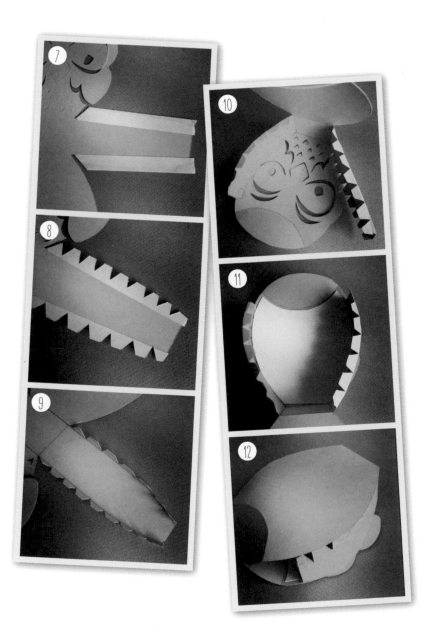

GIANT HAREBELL FAIRY LIGHTS

The whiteness of the bulbs in a string of LED lights creates a beautiful glow inside these pretty harebell-shaped fairy lights. Try white paper for snowdrops or yellow paper for cowslips.

SUPPLIES

Card, for template

A4 sheets of coloured paper, 80 gsm (1 sheet per lightbulb)

Pencil

Scissors

Glue stick

String of battery-powered LED fairy lights

makes 1 string

SAFETY NOTE
Although LED lights do not give out much heat, never leave them on overnight or unattended.

TO MAKE THE FLOWERS

1. Trace and cut the template on page 121 from card. Trim a sheet of coloured paper to a 21cm square.

2. Fold the paper square into quarters (run a ruler or your fingernails along each crease to get them really sharp). Place the folded paper on a clean, flat surface as a diamond shape, with the unfolded edges of the paper at the bottom.

3. Fold the right-hand side of the diamond into the centre. Repeat with the left-hand side to form a kite shape.

4. Open out the folds to make a diamond shape again. Place the template onto the folded paper as shown and trace around it.

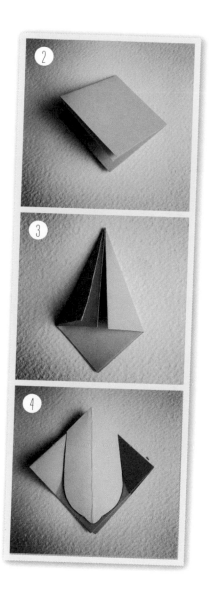

CONT. >>>

5. Using scissors, cut away the excess paper from the diamond shape.

6. Open the flower halfway and re-crease the small V-shaped fold at the top of each petal so it is sharp and will easily fold both ways.

7. Open out the flower and fold the V-shaped creases inwards to create valley folds (see pages 12-13 for an explanation of a valley fold).

8. Using a glue stick, spread glue over the valley folds of one petal and press it to the two petals on either side of it to make the flower shape. Repeat to join all four petals.

9. Your flat piece of paper should now be a bell shape.

10. Using scissors, curl the base of each petal upwards to form a flower-shaped paper shade.

11. Make as many paper flowers as there are bulbs in your string of fairy lights. Snip a small hole in the top of each paper shade and gently push each one onto a bulb.

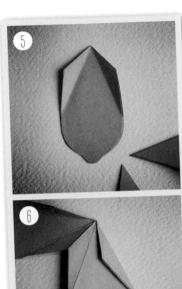
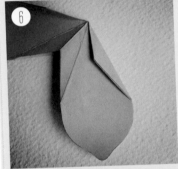

FOLK ART WALL STARS

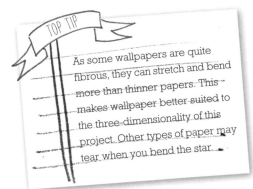

TOP TIP

As some wallpapers are quite fibrous, they can stretch and bend more than thinner papers. This makes wallpaper better suited to the three-dimensionality of this project. Other types of paper may tear when you bend the star.

These paper stars are reminiscent of the wooden good-luck symbols found in folk art. Using large sheets of card and offcuts of wallpaper means you can make the stars as big as you like.

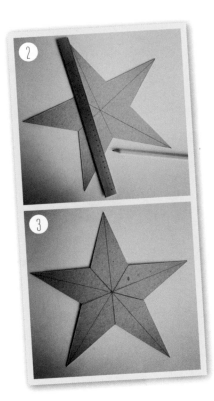

SUPPLIES

Pencil

Metal ruler

3mm thick grey card

Craft knife and cutting mat

Offcuts of wallpaper or other medium-weight paper

Spray adhesive

Double-sided tape

Hole punch or bradawl

Length of string or ribbon for hanging

Scissors

makes 1

TO MAKE THE STAR

1. Using the enlarged template on page 122 at your preferred size, trace the star outline onto the grey card. Using a pencil and ruler, draw the lines between the points of the star where indicated on the template.

2. Using a metal ruler and craft knife, cut out the star from the grey card. Turn the card over and draw pencil lines between the points of the star as before.

3. On one side of the star, score the five short lines marked in red on the template.

CONT. >>>

This Folk Art Star Garland is made from patterned paper, rather than covered card. Using the same template and method as the Folk Art Wall Stars, make a selection of paper stars in three different sizes – 15cm, 12cm and 9cm from point to point – scoring the lines on the reverse only. Arrange the paper stars in pleasing order and then pass a needle threaded with a length of cotton embroidery thread through one point of each star to cluster the stars together.

4. Turn the star over and score the five long lines marked in blue on the template.

5. With this side facing upwards, gently pinch and manipulate each star point until they become three-dimensional.

TO COVER THE STAR

6. Lay a piece of wallpaper right side down on a clean, flat surface. Spray the front of the star with spray adhesive, then place it on the wallpaper. Press the star flat. Cut around it, leaving a 2cm margin of wallpaper all the way round.

7. At each inner point of the star, trim away some of the wallpaper as shown. Place a strip of double-sided tape along each side of each star point. Remove its protective backing.

8. Fold the edges of the wallpaper back onto the double-sided tape, trimming away any excess at the tip of the star points.

9. Turn the star over and gently reshape it. Using a hole punch or bradawl, make a hole in the top of one of the star points and thread a length of string or ribbon through to make a hanging loop.

WATERLILY TABLE CENTRE

SUPPLIES

Card, for templates

A2 sheets of white or cream slightly translucent or patterned paper, approximately 120–180 gsm

Yellow translucent paper or tissue paper

Scissors

Craft knife and cutting mat

Metal ruler

Pencil

Glue stick

LED night lights

A1 sheet of green card, 210 gsm, for each leaf

makes 1

SAFETY NOTE:
Only use battery-operated LED night lights; never use a candle with a real flame.

Turn your dining table into a tranquil oasis by adding a selection of these light-up waterlilies. The LED night lights will flicker and cast beautiful shadows through the paper and luckily won't set fire to them!

TO MAKE THE FLOWERS

1. Trace and cut the enlarged templates on page 121 from card.

2. For the waterlily flowers, either trace around the card templates onto the white or cream paper and cut out using scissors, or place the card templates on the white paper and cut out using a craft knife. Cut out two large petals and two small petals per flowers.

CONT. >>>

3. Using the blunt back edge of the knife, score each petal of one large flower as indicated by the dotted line on the template. Fold up each petal. Repeat with all the flowers.

4. Place one of the large flowers on top of the other so the petals alternate. Glue in place.

5. Repeat with the small flowers, then glue the pair of small flowers in the centre of the large flower, again so the petals alternate.

6. Cut a 14 x 5cm rectangle from the yellow paper. Score a line 1.5cm from one long edge and cut rough points along it spaced approximately 2cm apart.

7. Snip straight cuts about 2.5cm deep and 5mm apart along the other long edge to make the stamens. Curl some of the stamens with the blade of the scissors (see page 13).

8. Roll from the short side of the rectangle to make a tube and join together with a little glue. Fold the rough points inwards, glue the underside of these and use them to fix the stamens to the centre of the waterlily. Finally place the LED night light in the centre.

TO MAKE THE BUD AND LEAVES

9. A bud is made by gluing the petals shut after a switched-on night light has been placed inside.

10. For the leaves, draw around a dinner plate onto the green card and cut out. Cut away a V shape with rounded corners at one side of the circle – like a slice of cake.

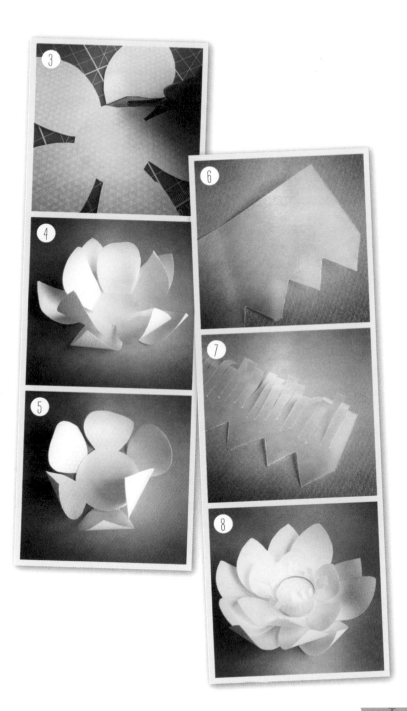

PAPER GARLANDS

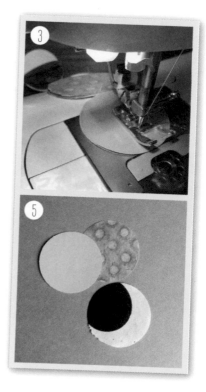

50mm diameter circle punch

Selection of medium-weight coloured and patterned papers

Sewing machine

Matching sewing thread

Scissors

Needle

Thin cream string or crochet cotton

Metal ruler

Craft knife and cutting mat

Glue stick

50mm diameter flower-shaped punch

makes 1 of each

EXTRA

For a different look, make a garland of spheres close to one another. Don't separate the paper stacks after step 4. Instead, just open them out to make them three-dimensional.

TO MAKE THE SPHERES GARLAND

1. Using the circle punch, cut out 30 discs from the coloured paper. If you are using handmade or fibrous paper, the punch may get stuck. Instead of punching the paper slowly as you would do normally, use a swift whack of the punch. It works much better!

2. Neatly stack three discs of different paper on top of each other. Repeat with all the discs.

3. Place one stack of discs centrally under the foot of your sewing machine. Slowly sew down the centre of the stack with long straight stitches.

4. When you reach the edge of the first stack of discs, stop the sewing machine and place another stack under the foot. Repeat until all the stacks are sewn together in a row.

5. Use scissors to separate the stacks. Take the top disc of one stack and fold its two edges towards each other to make it three dimensional. Repeat with the bottom disc. Repeat with all the stacks.

6. Using a needle with string or cotton, thread the top of each sphere onto the string so the spheres are equally spaced. Display them somewhere lovely.

TO MAKE THE FLAG GARLAND

1. Using a metal ruler and craft knife, cut 25mm wide strips the length of your sheets of paper.

2. Starting at one end of a strip, use scissors to cut two diagonal lines that meet at a point. Repeat this approximately 6cm further along the strip – it doesn't matter if the flags are different lengths. Repeat until you reach the end of the strip.

3. Using the blunt back edge of the craft knife and a ruler, score a line approximately 2cm down from the flag's point. Fold along the scored line, then unfold.

4. Place the flags on a clean, flat surface so they are equidistant from one another. Arrange them in a pleasing order.

5. Using a glue stick, smear a line of glue along the crease in each flag.

6. Leaving a tail end of approximately 20cm at both ends, lay a length of string or cotton through the middle of the row of flags. Fold the point of each flag over the string, lining them up neatly and securing them in place.

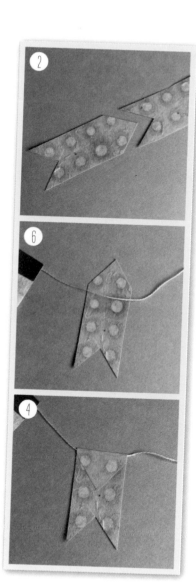

TO MAKE THE FLOWER GARLAND

1. Using the flower punch, cut out 50 flower shapes from the coloured paper.

2. Set half of the flowers aside. Place the other half on a clean, flat surface. Arrange the flowers so they are equidistant from one another and the colours and patterns are nicely mixed up.

3. Using a glue stick, place a spot of glue in the centre of each flower.

4. Leaving a tail end of approximately 20cm at both ends, lay a length of string or cotton through the middle of the row of flowers. Place a second flower from the half you set aside on top, lining the two up neatly and gluing them together. You can either match the pairs of flowers or vary the colours and patterns on each side of the garland. Repeat with all the flowers.

SHADOW TREE PICTURE

×●×●×●×⊙×⊙×⊛×●×⊙×●×●×⊙×●×⊛×●×

A box frame is perfect for these delicate papercut trees as it will not squash the picture and you get to see the pretty shadows cast by the trees. The background is effective whether you choose a plain contrasting colour, a pattern or simply go for white on white.

SUPPLIES

20cm square of medium-weight watercolour paper

20cm square box frame

Pencil

Metal ruler

Thin white paper

Masking tape

Craft knife and cutting mat

Hole punch

Scraps of coloured paper

Glue stick

Scissors

makes 1

TO MAKE THE TREE PICTURE

1. Mark out a 15.5cm square in the centre of the watercolour paper – this is the area that will be visible inside the frame. As box frames can vary, you may need to calculate the size of square that works for your particular frame. Instead of drawing lines to indicate the square, only make small pencil marks at each corner; that way there is less chance of the pencil marks being seen once the picture has been framed – which is more likely if the frame isn't quite square.

2. Trace and cut the template on page 122 from thin white paper. Place it face up in the centre of your drawn square and use masking tape to attach it to the watercolour paper.

CONT. >>>

80

3. Using a craft knife with a sharp blade, cut the tree shapes through the template and the watercolour paper. (Remember the solid line is where you cut; the dotted lines are for scoring and folding, which will be done later.) Cut slowly and carefully, especially when making the V-shaped cuts in the pine tree and the semi-circular cuts in the round bush. Use a ruler for super-straight tree trunks.

4. When all the trees have been cut, remove the template and carefully check your work. Re-cut any areas where your knife blade hasn't quite made it through both layers of paper, usually around the tips of the leaves. Use a hole punch to make a circular hole in the round tree.

5. Use a ruler and the back edge of your craft knife to score the trees along the dotted lines, then gently fold the cut halves of the trees back. Where the cut paper is quite narrow, use your knife blade like a shovel to help you turn and fold it.

6. Cut rectangles from the coloured-paper scraps, each rectangle just large enough for one tree. Use a glue stick to glue around the edge of each tree and carefully stick one piece of paper behind each tree. Make sure the coloured papers do not overlap much or the overlap will be seen behind the finished tree.

7. Turn the picture over and trim away the excess paper so the picture will fit into the box frame.

LIFESIZE CARDBOARD DEER

Momma Deer and Babba Deer make quick and effective decorations for winter festivities, but they're also fun to have around any time of the year. Make them any size. The only limit is the size of your cardboard boxes. Both are made the same way.

SUPPLIES

Large cardboard boxes

Pencil

Felt-tip pen

Metal ruler

Craft knife or scissors

Parcel or gaffer tape

Wide double-sided tape

makes 1 of each

TO MAKE THE DEER

1. These lifesize Momma Deer and Babba Deer each need two pieces of cardboard for their body and two for their head. Starting with the body, use a grid to enlarge the deer templates on page 114 and trace onto one piece of the cardboard box. On the grid shown, the scale is 1cm equals 7cm.

2. Cut out the cardboard using a craft knife or scissors. If using a craft knife, rest the cardboard on a suitable surface.

3. Place the cut-out body on top of the other piece of cardboard, draw around it and cut out the second body section.

4. Lay both sections on a flat surface so the upper edges are touching and the gridded sides are face up. Use lengths of parcel or gaffer tape to tape them together. This is the deer's spine. Trim away any excess tape.

5. Repeat steps 1–3 to make the two sections of the deer's head. Place both sections on a flat surface and tape them together along the top of the neck.

6. Attach strips of double-sided tape to the body where indicated on the template and fix the head to the body.

7. Enlarge and cut out the tail. Fold it in half where indicated and attach it to the deer's bottom with double-sided tape.

FEATHER MOBILE

I love all the bright colours in these mobiles and the way the feathers move in the breeze. It's also a great way to use up all your scraps of paper.

SUPPLIES

Pencil

Card, for templates

Spray adhesive

Selection of scraps of paper in various colours and patterns

Paperclip

Scissors

Needle

Selection of coloured cotton threads

14cm diameter wooden embroidery hoop

Tape measure

1.5cm wide washi tape or coloured masking tape

Strong cotton thread or embroidery thread, for hanging

makes 1

TO MAKE THE FEATHERS

1. Using the templates on pages 122–23, trace the four feather outlines onto card.

2. Spray the wrong side of one sheet of coloured paper with adhesive and glue it to a second sheet of coloured paper so that you have a double-sided sheet. Repeat with several sheets of paper so you have a mix and match of colours and patterns on each side.

3. Place a feather template on top of two or three pieces of double-sided paper and clip them together with a paper clip. Using scissors, cut out the feather shapes from the double-sided paper.

CONT. >>>

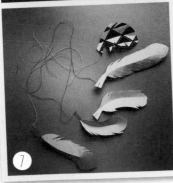

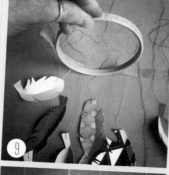

4. Repeat step 3 using the other templates until you have approximately 30 feathers.

5. Snip away little pieces of paper from the edge of the feathers for a real feather-like effect.

6. Score down the centre of each feather with the scissors, as shown on the templates and crease the feathers along the scored lines.

>>>

TO HANG THE FEATHERS

7. Using a needle, thread the end of each feather onto a length of cotton thread. Vary the lengths of thread so they measure between 5cm and 20cm.

8. Measure the circumference of the outside of the embroidery hoop. Cut a piece of washi tape or coloured masking tape to this length and lay it on a flat surface, sticky side up. Lay the lengths of cotton with their feathers along the tape so some feathers hang lower than others.

9. Roll the embroidery hoop along the tape from one end to the other. The hoop will pick up the tape and feathers as it goes.

10. Trim away any excess cotton and fold the excess washi tape over to the inside of the hoop.

11. To hang the mobile, cut two 50cm lengths of strong cotton or embroidery thread. Tie one end of one length to the hoop and the other end to the opposite side of the hoop. Repeat, attaching the second length of cotton to the other two quarter points of the hoop.

RUSTIC QUILLED DECORATIONS

Quilling is the art of rolling thin strips of paper into a variety of coils and shapes to make small intricate patterns. Using corrugated cardboard means you can supersize the quilled decorations, which are perfect for autumnal or winter festivities.

SUPPLIES

Roll of brown corrugated cardboard

Scissors

Ruler

Cookie cutters in heart shapes and other chosen shapes

Thin knitting needle

Glue dots

PVA glue

Ribbon, for hanging

Hairdryer

makes 1 heart and 1 snowflake

TO MAKE THE HEART SHAPE

1. Cut several strips 1cm wide from the corrugated card. Cut these strips into various lengths; the length of the strip determines the size of the coil – the longer the strip, the larger the coil.

2. Place a heart-shaped cookie cutter on a clean, flat surface. Holding the knitting needle in one hand, start winding a card strip tightly around the needle to create a coil.

3. Once the coil is the desired size, use a glue dot to fix the free end of the card strip to the coil. Slip the coil off the knitting needle and place it inside the cookie cutter. To make a coil with a more open centre, slip it from the knitting needle before gluing the free end in place, allow the coil to unravel slightly, then glue the end.

4. Make several different-size coils and place them inside the cookie cutter so it starts to fill up.

CONT. >>>

5. Once the cookie cutter is full of larger coils, start making smaller ones to fit into the gaps. Continue until the cookie cutter is completely filled.

6. Turn the cookie cutter over (the coils should be firmly held in place so they should not fall out) and place it back on your surface. Pat the coils down so they are level on the underside.

7. Cover the top of the coils with PVA glue, spreading it evenly so it covers all the coils. Try not to get glue on the cookie cutter as makes it harder to get the finished decoration out later. Allow to dry overnight.

8. Once completely dry, remove the decoration from the cutter. Use a craft knife to loosen any glue holding the coils to the cutter. If any coils fall out, simply glue them back in place.

9. Thread a length of ribbon through one of the open coils to hang the decoration.

TO MAKE THE SNOWFLAKE

These snowflake decorations do not rely on a cookie cutter to create the shape. Once you learn the basic shapes, you can create any pattern you like.

1. Cut seven 2 x 70cm strips from the corrugated card.

2. Roll one strip into a tight, round coil to form the centre of the snowflake. This coil should be approximately 3cm in diameter.

3. Make a crease in another strip, 20cm from one end. Roll a tight coil into this crease, then fix in place using a glue dot. Roll the rest of the strip into a relaxed coil around it.

4. Hold the coil tightly in one hand (between thumb and forefinger is easiest) and squash it into an oval shape approximately 6cm long (this may require a little adjustment of the relaxed coil to get the right size). Fix the free end in place with a glue dot.

5. Pinch the relaxed coil between your thumb and forefinger to create a teardrop shape.

6. Coat one side of the rounded half of the teardrop with PVA glue and hold it in place until it is tacky (a hairdryer helps speed this up). To make the other points of the snowflake, repeat steps 3–6.

7. Cut one of your 2 x 70cm strips into five 10cm lengths and roll these into tight coils. On a flat surface arrange the coils and teardrops into a snowflake shape.

8. Cover the snowflake with PVA glue, making sure you spread it over all areas where the coils and teardrops meet. Allow to dry overnight.

9. Once completely dry, thread a length of ribbon through the top point of the snowflake to hang or simply stand.

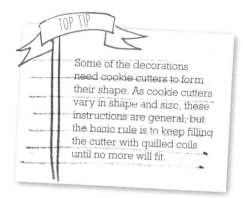

TOP TIP

Some of the decorations need cookie cutters to form their shape. As cookie cutters vary in shape and size, these instructions are general, but the basic rule is to keep filling the cutter with quilled coils until no more will fit.

SHIMMERING FISHES MOBILE

The variety of papers used to make the fish in this mobile all catch the light in different ways making it almost as mesmerising as if you were snorkelling alongside them. Colouring the watercolour paper with ink gives an added watery feel.

SUPPLIES

Selection of medium-weight papers, translucent, patterned, plain and watercolour

Hole punch

Circle cutter or 5cm circle punch

Large dinner plate

Medium-size paintbrush

Dark blue and turquoise ink

Kitchen roll

Sewing machine

Pale blue thread

makes 1

TO MAKE THE FISH

1. Using the templates on page 123, cut 17 fish from the various different papers.

2. Use a hole punch to make an eye in each of the paper fish roughly where indicated on the templates. Don't worry about being too accurate – it's better if the fish aren't all identical.

3. Fill a large dinner plate with cold water. Submerge each of the watercolour-paper fish in the water and leave to soak for 10 seconds.

CONT. >>>

4. Remove the fish from the water and place on a sheet of kitchen paper. Using the paintbrush dipped in ink, make a line along the belly edge of the fish; the ink will bleed up the paper to create a watery pattern. Allow to dry. If the paper fish has gone a bit wobbly from the water, once dry, press flat with a cool iron.

TO MAKE THE SPHERE

5. Using the circle cutter, cut three discs of paper.

TO CONSTRUCT THE MOBILE

6. Lay the fish out on a clean, flat surface and arrange them until you are happy with the order. Place some fish facing to the left and others facing to the right.

7. You are now going to machine-stitch all the fish together to form a long string. Leave a 30cm length of thread pulled through the sewing machine needle before stitching. This is for hanging the mobile. Place your first fish under the foot of the sewing machine so the needle is roughly in the centre of its spine. Sew slowly with long straight stitches. Just as you are coming to the belly edge of the first fish, stop the sewing machine, raise the foot and place the next fish so it butts up to the first. Lower the foot and continue sewing.

8. Repeat until you have stitched the last fish, then place the three discs of the sphere on top of each other, butting them up to the last fish. Stitch through the centre of the discs. Fan out the discs to make the sphere.

9. Using the 30cm thread, hang the mobile in a gentle breeze.

EXTRA!

You can make lots of different mobiles using this method, whether it's simply cutting 3 x 15cm strips from different papers or cutting individual letters to spell out a name.

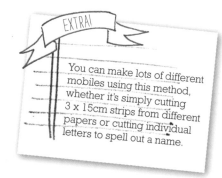

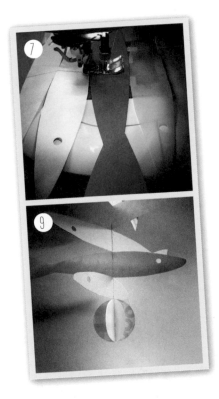

ROCOCO MIRROR FRAME

It's hard to believe that this mirror or picture frame is made from plain old brown paper. Its crisp lines and elegant curves belie its humble origins.

Old mirror or picture

Brown mount board

Pencil

Ruler

Craft knife

Cutting mat

PVA glue

Old piece of card or spatula

Brown paper

Flower punches in 2 sizes

Brown corrugated card

Silver and gold patterned paper

Spray adhesive

Thin brown card

Pinking shears

Glue gun

makes 1

TO MAKE THE FRAME

1. Place the mirror or picture you are making a frame for on the mount board and draw around it.

2. Measure and mark 1cm out and 2cm in from your drawn line to mark the cutting lines of the frame.

3. Using a craft knife and cutting mat, cut away the inside edge of the frame followed by the outside edge.

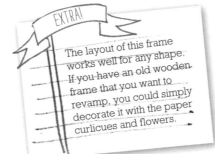

EXTRA!

The layout of this frame works well for any shape. If you have an old wooden frame that you want to revamp, you could simply decorate it with the paper curlicues and flowers.

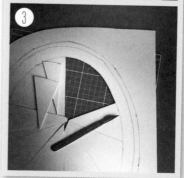

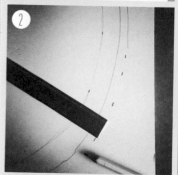

CONT. >>>

4. Cover the frame with a thin layer of PVA glue. First squeeze it on from the bottle, then spread it out evenly with an old piece of card or spatula.

5. Lay a piece of brown paper on a flat surface and place the frame, glue side down, on top.

6. Turn the frame over and smooth out any obvious lumps and creases. Little creases will vanish as the glue dries.

TO DECORATE THE FRAME

7. While the frame dries, make the paper flowers and curlicues. Use the flower punches or the daisy template from page 120 to cut five large flowers and ten small ones from the brown paper, corrugated card and silver and gold papers. Pinch each of the petals together to make the flowers three-dimensional.

8. Stick the brown paper to the thin brown card with spray glue. Using the templates from page 124, cut out one each of curlicues A, B and C. Flip the templates for curlicues A and B and cut a second set of curlicues that are a mirror image of the first.

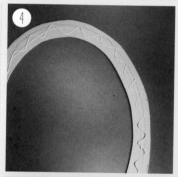

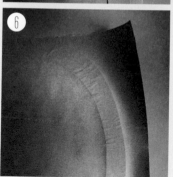

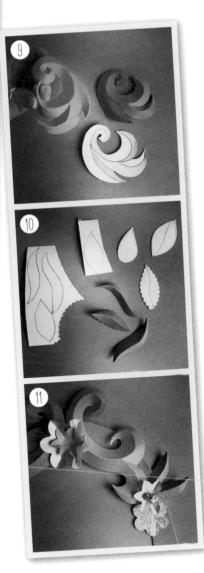

9. Score along the lines shown and carefully pinch the curlicues so they become three-dimensional. It is best to start at a point and work away from it, following each curve.

10. Use the templates to make the leaves. Cut some with pinking shears. Carefully fold each leaf along its spine to make it three-dimensional.

11. Start building up the frame. First trim the excess brown paper from the inside and outside edges of the frame, then place the largest curlicues at the top of the frame and the smaller ones at the bottom. Arrange the flowers and leaves around them. When you are happy with the design, use a glue gun to fix everything in place.

12. Scrunch up little pieces of paper to make the centres of flowers and attach them with the glue gun.

13. If you are fixing the frame to a mirror, you can use the glue gun directly onto the glass. If you are attaching it to a picture, use masking tape on the back of the picture.

GIANT GIFT ROSETTES

~~~~~~

A cluster of these supersized rosettes – usually made from shiny plasticised ribbon and used for decorating presents – makes an impressive wall display in your home or for a party. They are a great way of using up spare lengths of wallpaper.

Selection of lengths of wallpaper (see below)

Craft knife

Metal ruler

Cutting mat

Stapler

Double-sided tape

Ribbon or string

Sellotape

Using a craft knife, metal ruler and cutting mat, cut strips of wallpaper into the following lengths to make large, medium and small bows.

For a large rosette (50cm diameter)

One 10 x 40cm strip

Two 11 x 90cm strips

Four 11 x 1m strips

For a medium rosette (40cm diameter)

One 8 x 20cm strip

Two 9 x 70cm strips

Four 9 x 80cm strips

For a small rosette (24cm diameter)

One 5 x 15cm strip

Two 6 x 40cm strips

Four 6 x 50cm strips

makes 3 rosettes of different sizes

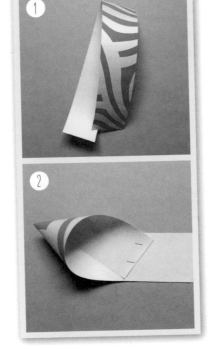

TO MAKE EACH ROSETTE

1. Fold one of the longest strips of wallpaper in half to find the centre.

2. Twist one end of the wallpaper strip so it meets the centre fold. Staple in place.

CONT. >>>

>>>

3. Repeat with the other end of the wallpaper strip.

4. Repeat steps 1–3 with another of the longest strips. Put two pieces of double-sided tape on the bottom of this second strip and fix it inside the first so the two are at right angles to each other. This makes the first layer of the rosette.

5. Repeat steps 1–3 with the other two longest strips, placing each one inside the first layer of the rosette and fixing them with double-sided tape as in step 4.

6. Repeat steps 1–4 with the two shorter strips and place these inside the rosette.

7. Roll the short strip of paper loosely and staple the ends together. Place some double-sided tape on the bottom and fix it in the centre of the rosette.

8. Attach a length of ribbon or string to the back of each rosette using strong Sellotape. Your rosette is now ready to hang on the wall.

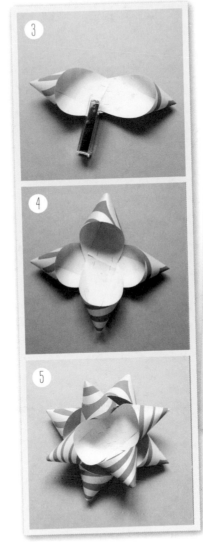

BOW GARLAND

I love this bow garland. It turns normal boring stationery supplies into something beautiful. (Though if the truth be told, I never find stationery supplies boring!)

Brown paper

Craft knife and cutting mat

Metal ruler

White, purple and neon yellow round stickers

White ring reinforcers

Pencil

Paperclips

Scissors

Glue sheet or double-sided tape

Glue dots

Needle

1m butcher's twine or embroidery thread in your chosen colour

makes 1

TO MAKE THE BOWS

1. For a garland approximately 240cm long, cut out thirty 20 x 22cm rectangles of brown paper. Decorate each with randomly placed coloured stickers and white ring reinforcers.

2. Fold one brown paper rectangle in half widthways and, using the template on page 123, trace the bow outline onto the paper with the centre of the bow is against the foldline.

3. Fold the remaining rectangles in half, as before. Stack three together, with the folds on the same side. Place the folded rectangle with the bow drawn on top, then paperclip all the sheets together to secure. Cut out the bow through all layers using scissors. It may be easier to use a craft knife to cut out the middle of the loops.

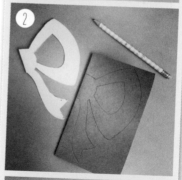

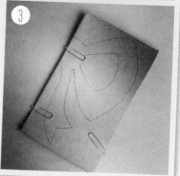

CONT. >>>

〉〉〉

4. Remove the paperclips and open out the bows. Repeat with the rest of the rectangles.

5. With one of the bows patterned side up, place a piece of glue sheet or a narrow strip of double-sided tape down its centre over the fold.

6. Place another bow on top, patterned side down. The two bows are now joined in the middle.

7. Repeat with the other bows until you have 15 pairs of bows, all with their patterned sides glued together.

TO CONSTRUCT THE GARLAND

8. Place one pair of bows on a clean, flat surface. Put a glue dot in the middle of both the left and right loops of the bow. Place another pair of bows on top, pressing firmly so the glue dots join the bows together.

9. Repeat, joining all the pairs of bows together. As you go, you will notice that when you lift the top bow up, the rest follow, like a concertina made of bows.

10. When you reach the last pair of bows, use a glue dot to join the left and right loops of the final bow to each other. Then pass the needle and butcher's twine or embroidery thread through the centre of the glue dot, leaving about 1m of twine for hanging the garland. Repeat at the other end of the garland.

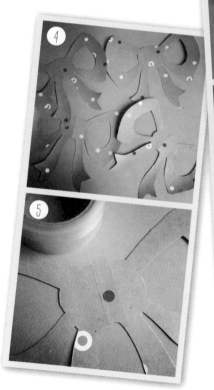

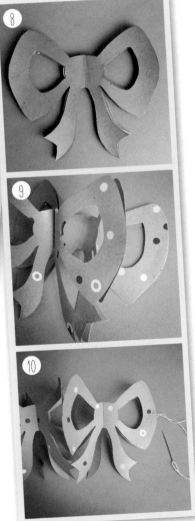

THE AMAZING AERIAL ACROBATS

Watch as Anna, Arabella and Adèle perform at death-defying heights, swaying in the breeze with their diamonds and pearls glistening in the spotlight.

SUPPLIES

For each acrobat

Pencil

Card, for templates

Craft knife and cutting mat

1 sheet of A4 medium-weight, double-sided flesh-coloured paper, for the body

Scraps of coloured and patterned paper, for the leotard, shoes and feathers

Glue stick

Self-adhesive jewels

Scissors

Narrow double-sided tape

Pinking shears or other decorative-edged scissors

6 × 26cm rectangle of coloured tissue paper

4 × 26cm rectangle of tissue paper in a second colour

Needle

Silver thread

For the moon girl

20cm square of double-sided gold card

makes 1 of each

TO MAKE EACH ACROBAT

1. Copy the templates on page 125 onto card and use a craft knife and cutting mat to cut out all the pieces from the coloured papers. If you are using paper that is only patterned on one side for the acrobat's shoes or leotard, make sure you get the paper the right way round so the pattern is on show.

TO MAKE THE FLYING GIRLS

2. To make either Anna or Arabella, the flying girls, use a glue stick to stick the leotard, hair and shoes in place.

3. Add self-adhesive jewels to her wrists, neck and headpiece. To make the feathers, fold each feather shape in half lengthways and snip away narrow triangles of paper.

CONT. >>>

4. To make the skirts, place a piece of double-sided tape across the flying girl's waist front and back, and trim it to the shape of her leotard. Remove the protective backing from the tape.

5. Trim one long edge of the larger rectangle of tissue paper with pinking shears or decorative-edged scissors. Starting at the flying girl's back, gather the tissue paper onto the double-sided tape, pressing it down to fix in place.

6. Repeat steps 4 and 5 with the smaller piece of tissue paper.

7. Glue the flying girl's belt to her skirt to cover up the raw edges.

8. To hang, run a needle and silver thread through the top of the flying girl's head and hang her from a hook or drawing pin in the ceiling.

TO MAKE THE MOON GIRL

9. To make Adèle the moon girl, repeat steps 1–3 then glue Adèle to her moon.

10. To make her train, cut an 8cm length of double-sided tape and place it on the work surface, sticky side up. Cut 6cm off the length of the narrower rectangle of tissue paper, trim with pinking shears or decorative-edged scissors all round and cut one end into a curve. Gather the tissue paper onto the double-sided tape.

11. Trim the wider rectangle of tissue paper so it is the same width as the smaller one. Remove the protective backing from the double-sided tape and gather the top third of this rectangle of tissue paper onto it. Gather the rest of the rectangle and attach it to Adèle's bottom with glue. Glue the heart over the top.

12. Hang by running a needle and thread through the top of the moon.

TEMPLATES

COLORADO CRITTERS
Page 14
These templates are actual size.
——— cut   – – – fold

LIFESIZE CARDBOARD DEER
Page 84
Referring to this grid, trace the deer body
and head outlines onto cardboard, enlarging
each 1cm square to 7cm square.

C

A   B

WOOLFIE
CUT 1 ON FOLD
OF PAPER

SNOW FOX
CUT 1 ON FOLD
OF PAPER

A
B

D   C

BABBA DEER
CUT 1 ON FOLD OF PAPER OR
CUT 2 FROM CARD (1 REVERSED)

MOMMA DEER
CUT 1 ON FOLD OF PAPER OR
CUT 2 FROM CARD (1 REVERSED)

B   A

C

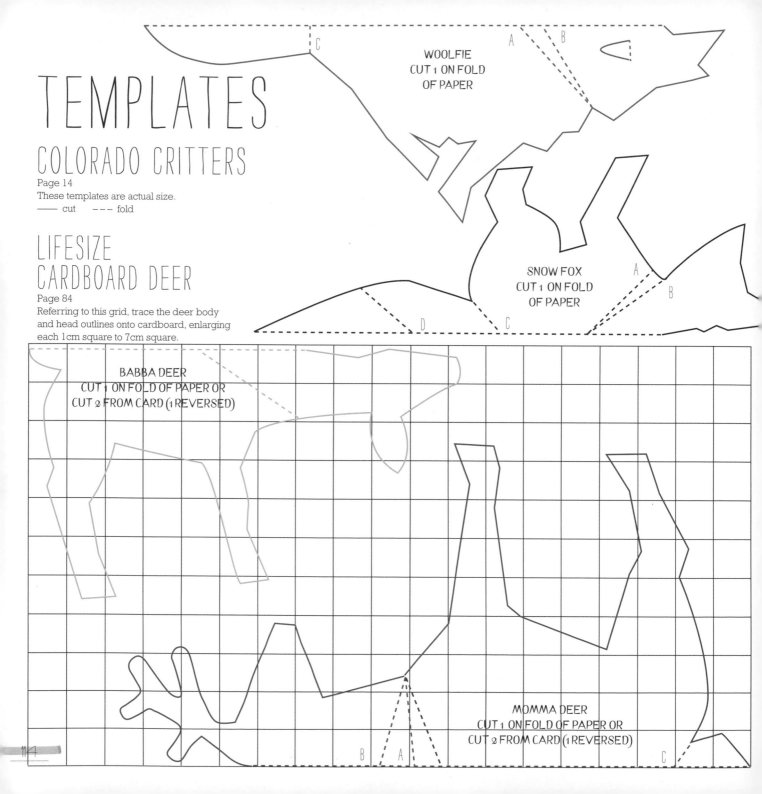

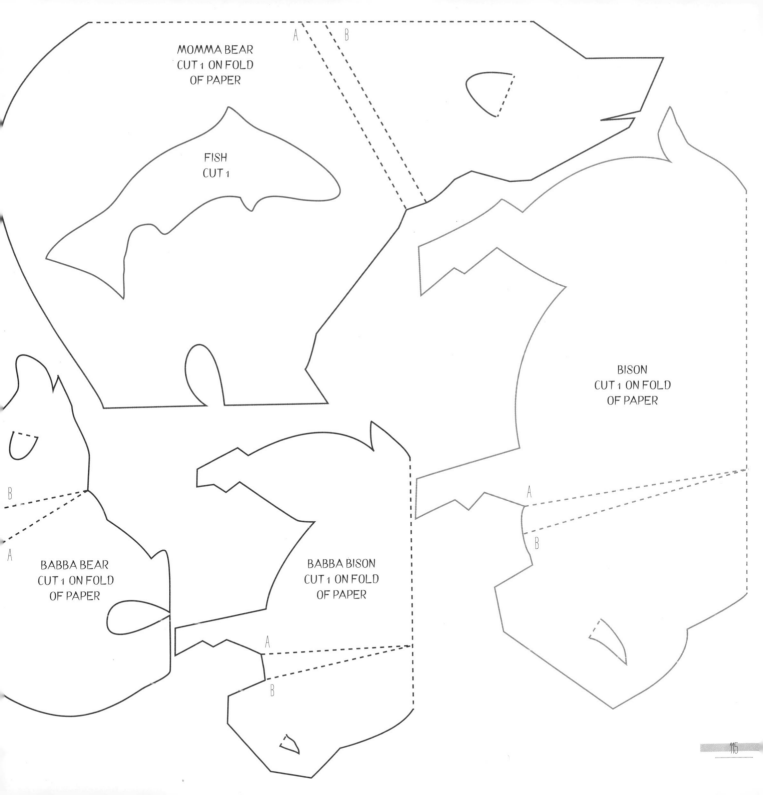

MOMMA BEAR
CUT 1 ON FOLD
OF PAPER

A

B

FISH
CUT 1

BISON
CUT 1 ON FOLD
OF PAPER

B

A

A

BABBA BEAR
CUT 1 ON FOLD
OF PAPER

BABBA BISON
CUT 1 ON FOLD
OF PAPER

A

B

A

B

115

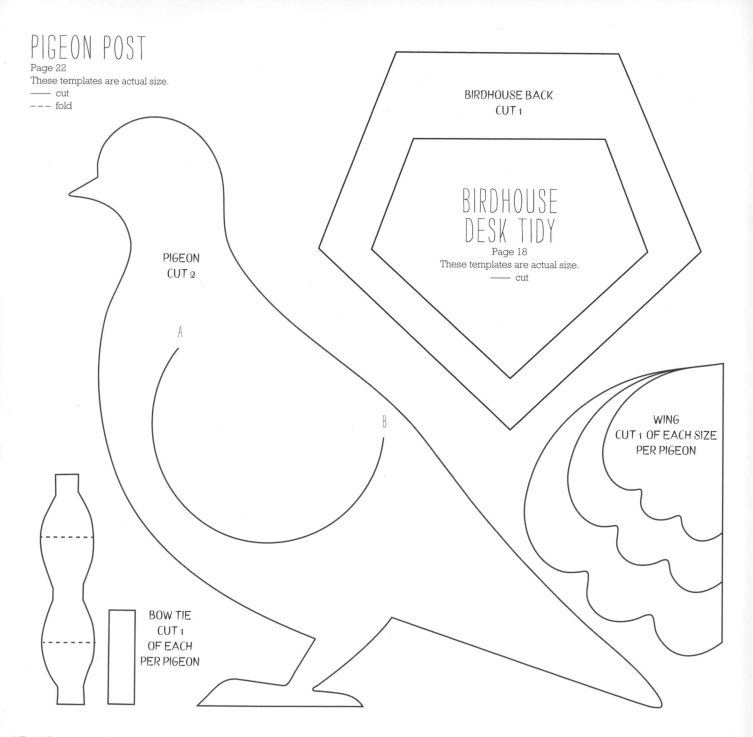

PIGEON POST

Page 22
These templates are actual size.
—— cut
––– fold

PIGEON
CUT 2

A

B

BOW TIE
CUT 1
OF EACH
PER PIGEON

BIRDHOUSE BACK
CUT 1

BIRDHOUSE
DESK TIDY
Page 18
These templates are actual size.
—— cut

WING
CUT 1 OF EACH SIZE
PER PIGEON

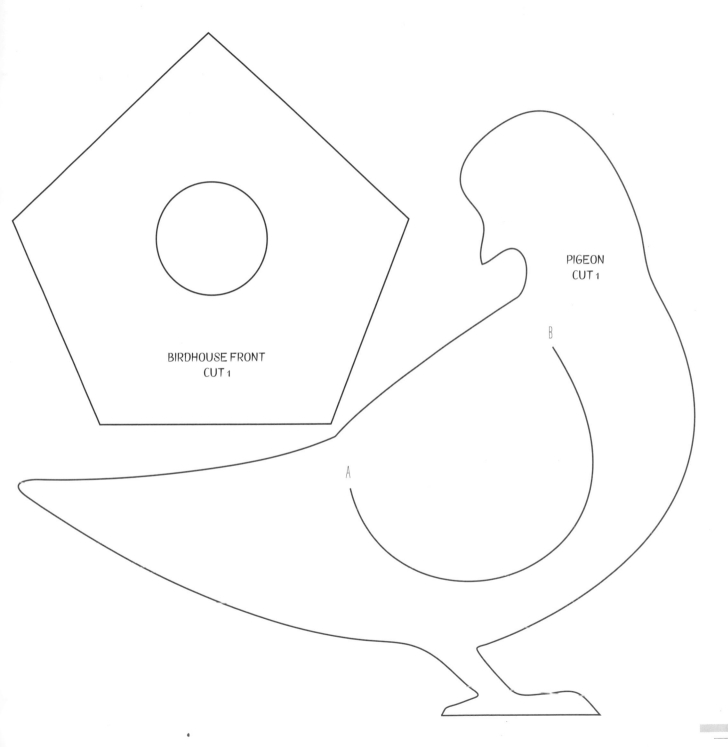

BIRDHOUSE FRONT
CUT 1

PIGEON
CUT 1

A

B

BIRDCAGE POP-UP CARD

Page 32
These templates are actual size.
—— cut - - - fold

BANNER
CUT 1

A B   B A

BIRD 1
CUT 1

BIRD 2
CUT 1

WING 1
CUT 1
PER BIRD

WING 2
CUT 1
PER BIRD

SMALL
AND LARGE
FLOWERS
CUT AS
MANY AS
NEEDED

BIRDCAGE
CUT 2 (1 REVERSED)

JAPANESE-BOUND NOTEBOOKS

Page 38

BOOK WITH RED BINDING

2 cm

1 cm
(from
the top) ← E

5 cm
(from
the top) ← D

9 cm ← C

13 cm ← B

17 cm ← A

BOOK WITH BLUE BINDING

1 cm

2 cm

1 cm
(from
the top) ← A

3 cm
(from
the top) ← B

5 cm
(from
the top) ← C

7 cm
(from
the top) ← D

9 cm ← E

11 cm ← F

13 cm ← G

15 cm ← H

17 cm ← I

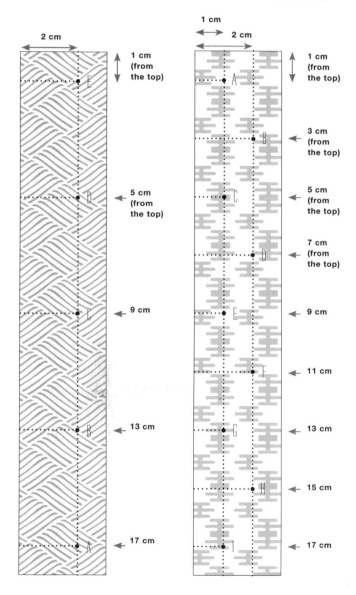

BOOK WITH BROWN BINDING

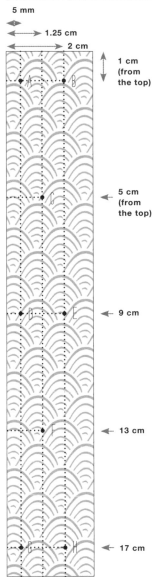

5 mm

1.25 cm

2 cm

1 cm
(from
the top)

5 cm
(from
the top)

← 9 cm

← 13 cm

← 17 cm

TO MAKE THE BOOK WITH BLUE BINDING

Follow steps 1-5 for the basic book block but refer to the binding guide for the blue book when marking out the drill holes. Thread the needle with the twine and starting at the top of the book begin binding.

1. Enter hole A from the rear of the book, take the twine around the spine of the book and back into hole A from the rear.

2. Enter hole B from the front of the book, take the twine around the spine of the book and back into hole B from the front.

3. Enter hole C from the rear of the book, take the twine around the spine and back into hole C from the rear.

4. Enter hole D from the front of the book, take the twine around the spine and back into hole D from the front.

5. Enter hole E from the rear of the book, take the twine around the spine and back into hole E from the rear.

6. Continue this process until you reach hole I (when you should be coming from the rear). Wrap the twine around the spine then travel back up the book, filling in the missing stitches. Tie a knot in the twine between holes A and B and neatly trim the ends.

TO MAKE THE BOOK WITH BROWN BINDING

Follow steps 1–5 for the basic book block but refer to the binding guide for the brown book when marking out the drill holes. You may want to make the drill holes slightly larger as the needle does pass through each hole a few times. Thread the needle with the twine and starting at the top of the book begin binding.

1. Enter hole A from the rear of the book, take the twine around the spine and back into hole A from the rear.

2. Enter hole C from the front of the book, take the twine around the spine and back into hole C from the front.

3. Enter hole D from the rear of the book, take the twine around the spine and back into hole D from the rear.

4. Enter hole F from the front of the book, take the twine around the spine and back into hole F from the front.

5. Enter hole G from the rear of the book, take the twine around the spine and back into hole G from the rear.

6. Enter hole H from the front of the book, take the needle and twine up to F entering from the rear.

7. Enter hole E from the front of the book, come out at hole C entering from the rear.

8. Enter hole B from the front of the book, come out at hole A entering from the rear.

9. Enter back into hole B from the front then out at hole C entering from the rear.

10. Enter hole E from the front then out at hole F entering from the rear.

11. Enter hole H from the front then across to hole G entering from the rear.

12. Enter hole F from the front then up to hole D entering from the rear.

13. Enter hole C from the front then tie the threads together between holes A and C at the back of the book.

ANEMONE AND CAMELLIA BOUQUET

Page 46
These templates are actual size.
—— cut

FLORAL GIFT GARLAND

Page 50
These templates are actual size.
—— cut – – – fold

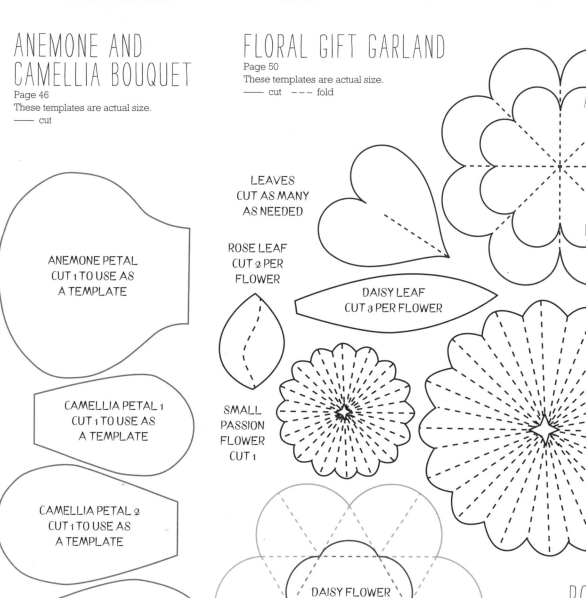

ANEMONE PETAL
CUT 1 TO USE AS
A TEMPLATE

CAMELLIA PETAL 1
CUT 1 TO USE AS
A TEMPLATE

CAMELLIA PETAL 2
CUT 1 TO USE AS
A TEMPLATE

CAMELLIA PETAL 3
CUT 1 TO USE AS
A TEMPLATE

LEAVES
CUT AS MANY
AS NEEDED

ROSE LEAF
CUT 2 PER
FLOWER

DAISY LEAF
CUT 3 PER FLOWER

SMALL
PASSION
FLOWER
CUT 1

DAISY FLOWER
CUT 1 OF EACH
SHAPE

A
C
B
D

PETALS CUT
AS MANY AS
NEEDED IN
EACH SIZE

LARGE
PASSION
FLOWER
CUT 1

ROSE, PASSION FLOWER & DAISY GIFT TAGS

Page 54–58
These templates have been scaled down to fit on
the page. To use the template, simply photocopy
the sample at 200%.
—— cut – – – fold

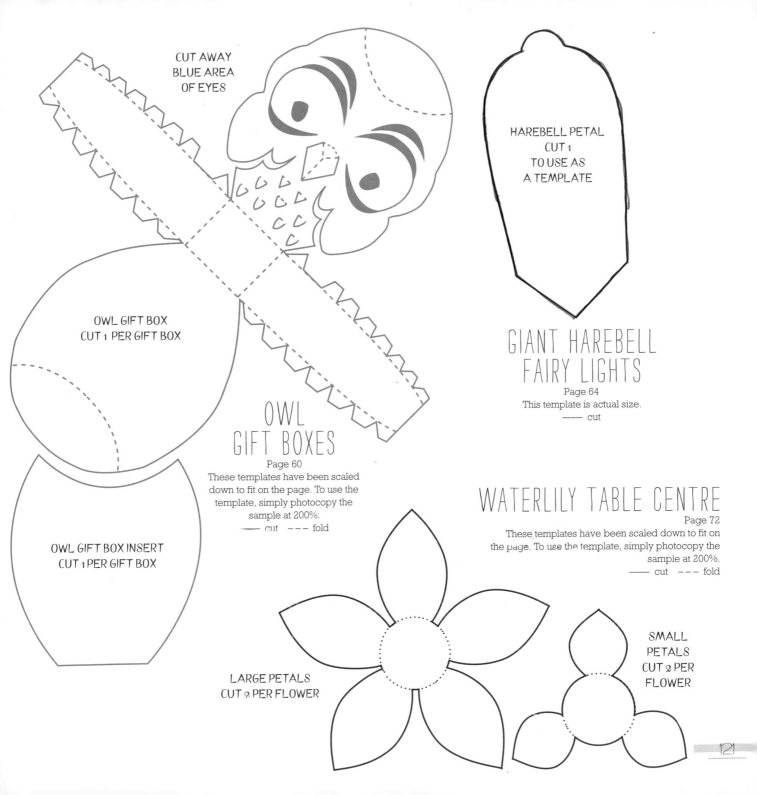

CUT AWAY
BLUE AREA
OF EYES

HAREBELL PETAL
CUT 1
TO USE AS
A TEMPLATE

OWL GIFT BOX
CUT 1 PER GIFT BOX

GIANT HAREBELL
FAIRY LIGHTS
Page 64
This template is actual size.
—— cut

OWL
GIFT BOXES
Page 60
These templates have been scaled
down to fit on the page. To use the
template, simply photocopy the
sample at 200%.
—— cut – – – fold

OWL GIFT BOX INSERT
CUT 1 PER GIFT BOX

WATERLILY TABLE CENTRE
Page 72
These templates have been scaled down to fit on
the page. To use the template, simply photocopy the
sample at 200%.
—— cut – – – fold

LARGE PETALS
CUT 2 PER FLOWER

SMALL
PETALS
CUT 2 PER
FLOWER

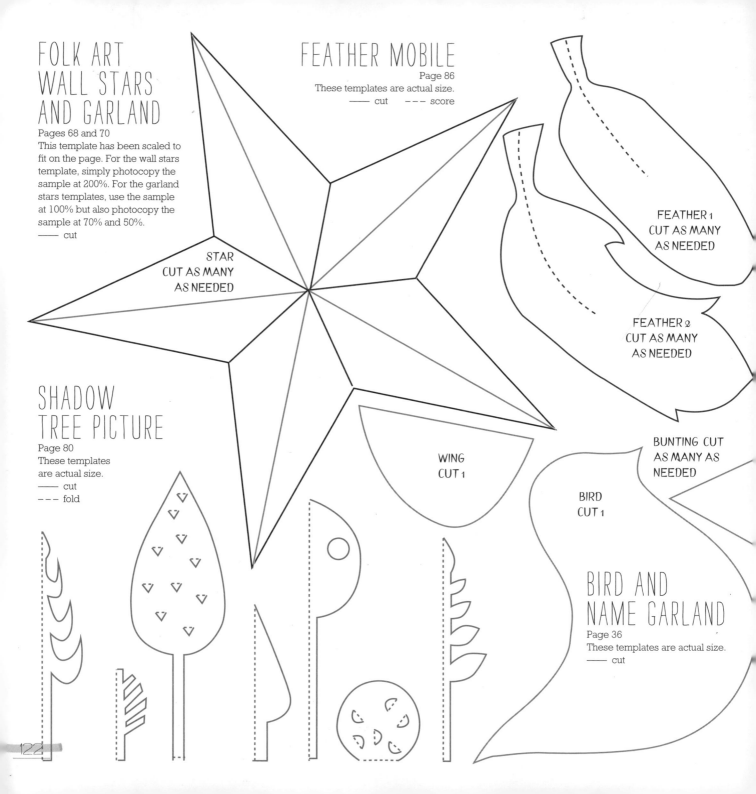

FOLK ART WALL STARS AND GARLAND

Pages 68 and 70
This template has been scaled to fit on the page. For the wall stars template, simply photocopy the sample at 200%. For the garland stars templates, use the sample at 100% but also photocopy the sample at 70% and 50%.

—— cut

STAR
CUT AS MANY
AS NEEDED

FEATHER MOBILE

Page 86
These templates are actual size.

—— cut   --- score

FEATHER 1
CUT AS MANY
AS NEEDED

FEATHER 2
CUT AS MANY
AS NEEDED

SHADOW TREE PICTURE

Page 80
These templates are actual size.

—— cut
--- fold

WING
CUT 1

BUNTING CUT
AS MANY AS
NEEDED

BIRD
CUT 1

BIRD AND NAME GARLAND

Page 36
These templates are actual size.

—— cut

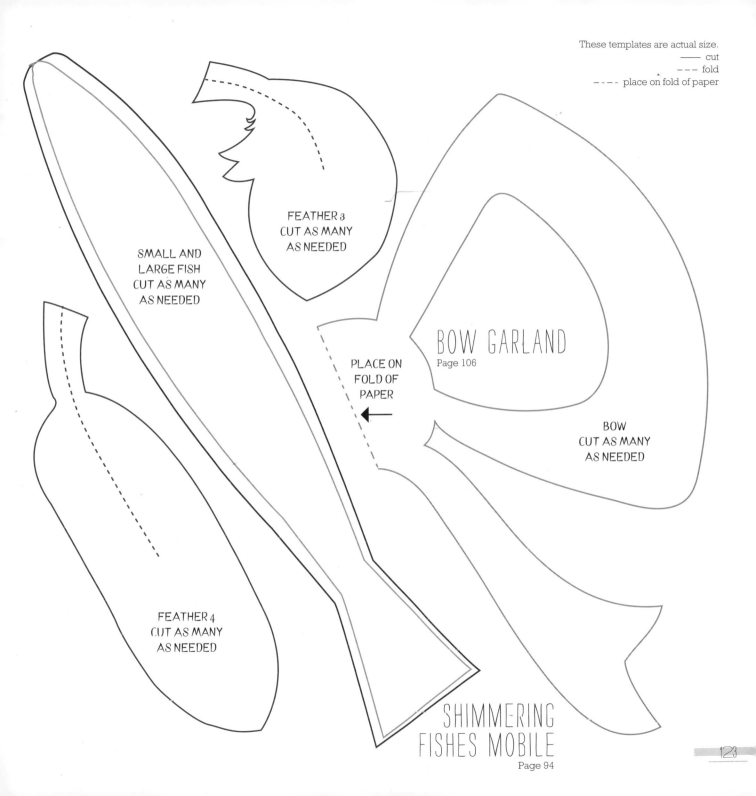

These templates are actual size.
—— cut
– – – fold
-- -- place on fold of paper

FEATHER 3
CUT AS MANY
AS NEEDED

SMALL AND
LARGE FISH
CUT AS MANY
AS NEEDED

BOW GARLAND
Page 106

PLACE ON
FOLD OF
PAPER

BOW
CUT AS MANY
AS NEEDED

FEATHER 4
CUT AS MANY
AS NEEDED

SHIMMERING
FISHES MOBILE
Page 94

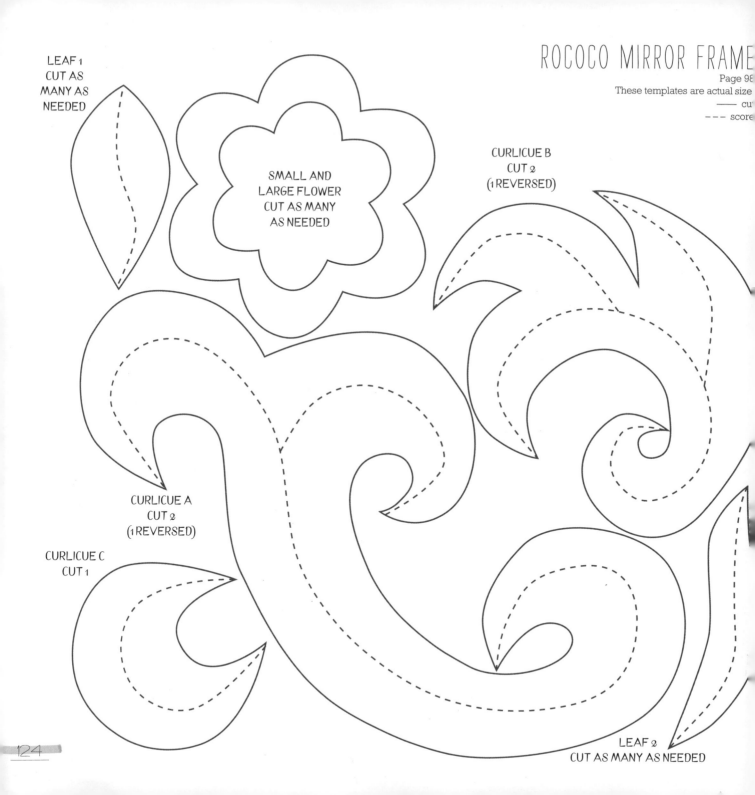

LEAF 1
CUT AS
MANY AS
NEEDED

SMALL AND
LARGE FLOWER
CUT AS MANY
AS NEEDED

CURLICUE B
CUT 2
(1 REVERSED)

CURLICUE A
CUT 2
(1 REVERSED)

CURLICUE C
CUT 1

LEAF 2
CUT AS MANY AS NEEDED

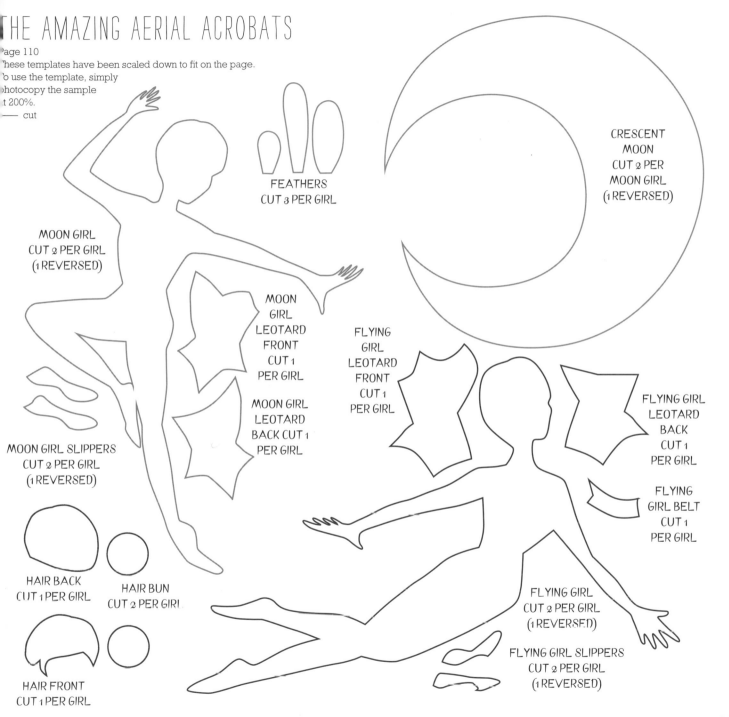

THE AMAZING AERIAL ACROBATS

Page 110
These templates have been scaled down to fit on the page.
To use the template, simply
photocopy the sample
at 200%.
—— cut

FEATHERS
CUT 3 PER GIRL

CRESCENT
MOON
CUT 2 PER
MOON GIRL
(1 REVERSED)

MOON GIRL
CUT 2 PER GIRL
(1 REVERSED)

MOON
GIRL
LEOTARD
FRONT
CUT 1
PER GIRL

FLYING
GIRL
LEOTARD
FRONT
CUT 1
PER GIRL

MOON GIRL
LEOTARD
BACK CUT 1
PER GIRL

FLYING GIRL
LEOTARD
BACK
CUT 1
PER GIRL

FLYING
GIRL BELT
CUT 1
PER GIRL

MOON GIRL SLIPPERS
CUT 2 PER GIRL
(1 REVERSED)

HAIR BACK
CUT 1 PER GIRL

HAIR BUN
CUT 2 PER GIRL

FLYING GIRL
CUT 2 PER GIRL
(1 REVERSED)

FLYING GIRL SLIPPERS
CUT 2 PER GIRL
(1 REVERSED)

HAIR FRONT
CUT 1 PER GIRL

RESOURCES

ARJOWIGGINS CREATIVE PAPERS
arjowigginscreativepapers.com
Paper suppliers. Great website full of
inspiration and offering a sample service.

ARTBOX
artbox.co.uk
Cute Japanese stationery, notebooks,
erasers and stickers.

BLADE RUBBER
bladerubberstamps.co.uk
12 Bury Place, London WC1A 2JL
020 7831 4123
A beautiful shop choc-full of stamps, inks
and scrapbooking supplies.

COWLING AND WILCOX
cowlingandwilcox.com
Large art shop with five London branches.

FREE ONLINE FONTS
There are lots of websites with free fonts to
download. For starters, try …
dafont.com
fontsquirrel.com

HOBBYCRAFT
hobbycraft.co.uk
A nationwide hobby and craft superstore.
Just brilliant.

ELLA JOHNSTON
ellajohnston.wordpress.com
Beautiful art and illustration, and supplier of
the bird pictures featured in this book.

LAURA ASHLEY
lauraashley.com
Lovely wallpapers that are perfect for the
projects in this book.

LIBERTY
liberty.co.uk
Regent Street, London W1B 5AH
Shop with an inspiring stationery
department.

MUJI
muji.com
A good place for small metal rulers and
Perspex storage solutions that are great
for keeping your papers organised. Stores
nationwide.

PAPERCHASE
paperchase.co.uk
213–215 Tottenham Court Road, London
W1T 7PS .
The London flagship store on Tottenham
court road has so many papers it's
ridiculous. Also sells lovely stationery.

PRESENT AND CORRECT
presentandcorrect.com
23 Arlington Way, London EC1R 1UY
The shop and online store that feeds my
printed paper addiction. This is where to
buy vintage German sausage packaging
and old exercise books.

PULLINGERS ART SHOP
pullingers.com
Good online art suppliers with three shops
in Surrey.

RAINBOW FLORIST SUPPLIES
rainbowfloristsupplies.co.uk
For crepe paper and other floristry goodies.

RODDY AND GINGER
roddyandginger.co.uk
A print-maker selling great wallpaper and
with a beautiful home.

RYMAN
ryman.co.uk
The place for office supplies like hole
reinforcers and gold stars. Stores nationwide.

G.F. SMITH
gfsmith.com
Paper suppliers offering lots of helpful
tips on choosing the right paper for your
project. Also provides samples.

TASHTORI ARTS AND CRAFTS
facebook.com/pages/TashTori-Arts-and-
Crafts/214629638549591
29 Station Street, Lewes BN7 2DB
01273 48670
Lewes-based art shop; good paper and
scrapbooking suppliers.

TIGER
tigerstores.co.uk
Like Ikea only better. Sells home
accessories, craft supplies and general
knick-knackery.

WASHI TAPES
washitapes.co.uk
For all your washi tape needs.

INDEX

THANK YOU THANK YOU THANK YOU

Thanks to all at Quadrille, especially Lisa, Claire and Chinh. And thank you to Hilary and Gemma for making the book make sense and look beautiful.

To lovely Keiko for more amazing photography, calmness and general patience.

To all my family, Mum for her general brilliance, Dad for his remarkable prop making, Jo for her paper skills suggestions, Ian and the boys always inspiring me with their handmade cards and gifts, Auntie and Uncle, Nanny and Grandad for their support, belief, encouragement and suggestions.

Thank you Elias and Barry for allowing me a supermarket sweep for props from your inspiring home.

Love to Jake, Kirsty, Laura, Hannah (both of them) for listening to my ramblings, half finished sentences and general maniacal behaviour.

To Rhiannon, who knew that when we had our little stall at the school craft fair it would lead to this?!

Publishing Director Jane O'Shea
Creative Director Helen Lewis
Commissioning Editor Lisa Pendreigh
Editor Hilary Mandleberg
Design & Art Direction Claire Peters
Designer Gemma Wilson
Photographer Keiko Oikawa
Stylist and Illustrator Christine Leech
Production Director Vincent Smith
Production Controller Aysun Hughes

Quadrille *craft*

www.quadrillecraft.com

First published in 2013 by
Quadrille Publishing Ltd
Alhambra House
27–31 Charing Cross Road
London WC2H 0LS
www.quadrille.co.uk

Text, project designs, artwork & illustrations
© 2013 Christine Leech
Photography
© 2013 Keiko Oikawa
Design & layout
© 2013 Quadrille Publishing Ltd

The designs in this book are copyright and must not be made for resale.

British Library Cataloguing-in-Publication Data
A catalogue record for this book is available from the British Library.

ISBN: 978 184949 307 9

Printed in China.